T0147085

What people are saying about *Prosperity/Gospel*

Prosperity/Gospel is a testimonial of what one person found as they moved into an immersion of the Gospel in their lives. Adam Sculnick lifts up the pain of his life as well as the search for meaning and purpose and finds "it's not about me." Adam desires to help others who follow him to navigate some key questions and answers in the Gospel. With a very readable style and vivid illustrations, Adam points to a pathway for other seekers and searchers to find meaning in the "big story" of God and His love for us. It is a book that can serve as part of personal devotionals and for group study as we all find out how our stories relate to God's Story!

Jul Medenblik
President, Calvin Theological Seminary

This book will be a great help to your everyday life—if you know Jesus or do not. Adam's work here is rooted in his personal journey from what I term a "cotton candy worldview" that saw Adam as the center of his world, to a Jesus-centered worldview rooted in the power of the Bible, God's Word. Adam's purpose in this book is important that everyone hear. My life should be centered on Jesus—not me. In a world—and even among many Christians—that says "satisfy yourself," Adam challenges his readers to listen to Jesus's promises and not the empty promises of a prosperity message. His thoughtful study questions at the end of each chapter are grown from a life lived before Christ and now in Christ. They are real and helpful, and help me interact with the Bible. On top of that, his biblical and theological analysis of the prosperity message are spot on. So is his prescription for addressing it. Many churches, particularly American ones, are preaching for comfortable lives rather than for changing lives. Jesus said He came to seek and to save the lost (Luke 19:10). That's Adam's heart here. If you don't know Jesus, trade the empty promises of culture and surrender to Jesus. If you do know Jesus, give up quoting the Bible like a fortune cookie and looking at God like Santa Claus—bend the knee at the empty tomb. Live life for His glory and not yours. Thanks to Adam for a very timely word. I recommend *Prosperity/Gospel* to all who seek to deepen their faith in the area.

Dave Eppling
Director of Presidential Projects; Truett McConnell University

It is refreshing to find a millennial author who calls Christians back to basic and fundamental Christian teachings as actually espoused in the Gospel of the Bible. We Christians are not to place ourselves at the center of our lives but to seek out God's perfect will, not our own. Boomer Christians have for too long espoused leveraged materialism for their own misplaced security. The mindset should be on sowing the Gospel, not reaping it with bigger budgets and more bricks and mortar. Our prosperity rightly focused should be primarily a *spiritual* prosperity, placing love of God and neighbor ahead of self as we aspire to be holy as God is holy. The author reminds us not to be inwardly focused on self but rather outwardly focused, with a balance by and between our mental, physical, social, emotional, and spiritual capacities along with our financial self.

Dr. Thomas Seel, MBA
Executive Director of Operations and Finance, Multiply222Network
Instructor, graduate Christian Worship classes at Liberty University

PROSPERITY/GOSPEL expresses quite clearly how it is that we can be sucked into the wrong message from false teachers. I like the way Adam describes the prosperity gospel as a disease and then shows how it results in spiritual dis-ease. This book speaks to a topic that is rarely discussed in such depth and I commend him for his desire to help us all to grasp the issues. Readers who reflect on the questions posed at the end of each section will be faced with their own reality and hopefully be able to reconstruct their beliefs where necessary.

Ash Adams
Author; Lambent Light: Who Will Know Their Name?

PROSPERITY/ GOSPEL

············· What's Your Story? ·············

True gospel, false gospel, and the truth that
you are not the main character in a book about you
but a supporting character in a book about God

ADAM SCULNICK

WESTBOW
PRESS®
A DIVISION OF THOMAS NELSON
& ZONDERVAN

WestBow Press books may be ordered through booksellers or by contacting:

WestBow Press
A Division of Thomas Nelson & Zondervan
1663 Liberty Drive
Bloomington, IN 47403
www.westbowpress.com
844-714-3454

ISBN: 978-1-6642-6630-8 (sc)
ISBN: 978-1-6642-6631-5 (hc)
ISBN: 978-1-6642-6629-2 (e)

Library of Congress Control Number: 2022908592

Print information available on the last page.

WestBow Press rev. date: 05/19/2022

To Amber Sculnick,

my beautiful wife, ceaseless supporter, and best friend,

thank you for never giving up on me, even

when I made it so very hard.

I love you, and I thank God for you every day.

You show me the Grace of God in a way nobody else ever could.

To Aiden, Jackson, and Delilah,

the blessings I could never have expected

and can't imagine being without,

I'm so grateful to be your dad.

And finally, to Dave and Lea Eppling,

who saw who I was in Christ long before I did.

May God raise up a generation of men and women
who are passionate for the truth of the gospel.

Contents

Preface

When you've set out to write a book, it's important to understand the answers to a few major questions. Who is the book about? Why am I writing it? What message do I want to convey? How do I want my reader to feel and behave following their reading of my book? Other than the first, the rest of these questions in fact are the very last things I cared about—until December 26, 2017. It was a Tuesday, and I'll never forget it. Until that day, I had lived as most people do, under the assumption that life is a book written about me—that I am the main character, and everyone around me is in a supporting role of some kind.

There were other people in my life who were important to me. I had a beautiful wife who'd been at my side for ten years, and we had three children. In fact, they were of paramount importance to me, and I would have done anything for them at the time—and still would. The struggle, if I'm honest, is that what I just said was only half true. I believed that I loved them 100%, but if push came to shove, only the hero of the story has to live, and I'm the main character, not them. See the problem?

The mission of *Prosperity/Gospel* is to clarify what I see as a truly infectious disease of Christendom that is spreading. When we believe that each of us is the main character in the book of life, we too easily fall into alignment with the false teachings of preachers who call themselves Christian, stand at the pulpit, and preach what is now commonly referred to as "prosperity gospel." It is extremely appealing to a world that lives in excess, a world that loves itself and thinks it is the center of things. But it is a disease.

God desires our prosperity, yes. And by the end of this book, you'll know that to be true and what it means—not because I said so, but because He says so.

In order to write this book in a meaningful way, I had to begin by acknowledging that the only book that can really tell you how to live is not this one. Don't believe something I say? Fact-check me with the Bible. That's the only book that can tell you how to live and who the main character in your life really is. The point of my book is to point you to *the* Book—not to point you to people who preach from it nor to glorify me as an author, but to point you right to the Word.

I hope you take away a good deal of food for thought from this book, and toward that end, I've concluded each chapter with a set of questions for your reflection. But in so far as books can help you, it's not this one you should get really into. It's His. It's the Bible. So I pray that this book would lead you to a deeper desire to encounter God's word in the Bible. As an aid, I've included a section in the back of this book called "Scriptures Cited" where you can see the complete biblical texts that I've referenced throughout the book, in order of appearance. If you don't have a bible, you can look in the back to see the truth of God's word, but I always suggest a bible be near by when reading something that makes reference to it. And ultimately, all of those texts should be read in their context, meaning with the parts written before and after them, so please do, if you don't already, grab a bible.

OK, so I've told you why I wrote this book, and I think it's important also to tell you why you should read it. Why should anybody read it, really? Is this going to be one of those books by some author you've never met telling you that you're doing life wrong? No. Is this me telling you how I do things and to follow my lead? No. This is me feeling very much that God has been preparing me to share this story. I've felt this way for a long time. And I can't help but feel that a number of people are in the same place I was. Maybe you?

I subtitled the book *What's Your Story?* but now I'm telling you it isn't your story at all, while here I am getting ready to tell you a story about me. "What's the deal, Adam?" you may be asking. The deal is this: we are focused big-time on ourselves. But it isn't a story about us. And the longer we make it out to be, the longer we go on feeling that something is missing. Like we just can't get to the place we want to. And that feels wrong, because the hero in every story is the element that moves the story forward. If we are stuck, the world should be too, and yet everyday life goes on.

What I want you to see is that the world goes on because *you* are not the focal point. You are not the main character. God is the main character. My hope is that you begin to see more and more, as I have, that the story *involves* you but isn't *about* you. It's about seeing your role and embracing it.

And what is that role? I'll unpack that a lot in the chapters to come, but right now I want to tell you how I got to this point.

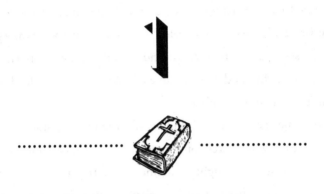

In The Beginning.
My Beginning

I was raised as an only child by a single mother who by all accounts
was absent—sometimes for work, other times for leisure, but absent
nonetheless. My father was *completely* absent—as in, living in another
country and never making contact. As a result, I became independent
from an early age. That continued, or perhaps I should say worsened,
through my rebellious youth and young adulthood. I was very self-
destructive in more ways than one, as a teen and never really grew
out of it. I may have kicked the habits I'd formed, but not the self-
serving nature within myself that led to forming those habits in the
first place. My self-destructiveness truly came to a head when I ran
my business into the ground in the aftermath of an affair I had with a
client—a story perhaps not for this book but nevertheless important

to touch on, if only as to underscore the self-indulgent, self-centered life I was leading.

As I look back, two things through all of that are painfully clear. The first is that I was most definitely the main character and sought first and foremost to develop myself and my story, as any good protagonist should. The second, and infinitely more important, is that God was alive and working in each of the moments leading up to that Tuesday in December.

The major issue with thinking you're the main character is that you assume the world owes you something. And though not everyone will admit to such a haughty statement, the truth is embedded in their actions, or rather in their reactions to the things of the world. Jeremiah 17:9 (ESV) tells us, "The heart is deceitful above all things, and desperately sick; who can understand it?"

So who are we kidding really but ourselves when we think that we *aren't* our own main character? And here's the kicker, laid out so clearly in 1 John 2:15–17 (ESV):

> Do not love the world or the things in the world. If anyone loves the world, the love of the Father is not in him. For all that is in the world—the desires of the flesh and the desires of the eyes and pride in possessions— is not from the Father but is from the world. And the world is passing away along with its desires, but whoever does the will of God abides forever.

When we really focus on the world, what we are saying is that it is the source of our gratification. And if that is the case, then we believe we *are* the main character, because the world wouldn't be giving us things if we didn't hold the most important seat.

The truth is, the world is full of ancillary characters in a story about God. It always has been from Genesis 1 and will continue to be until Revelation 22. He is working all things out for our good and His glory (see Romans 8:28). Notice that I didn't say that *we* are working all things out for our good *through* His glory, or that He is working *for us and our glory*. I didn't say those things because the Bible doesn't say those things, even if some church leaders say it does. And the way we know He is working all things out is by getting to know Him better through His word.

The rallying cry of the Protestant Reformation was the Latin phrase *sola scriptura*, scripture alone. My friends, only scripture can show you how to really live. If it isn't in the Bible, it isn't God's Word, and if it isn't God's Word, then it is secondary. We live in a world where the secondary is focused on as primary, and the true primary, God, is made less than. Let's be clear: all the things we have, all the things we want to have or long to have, are secondary to that which is found in His Word. As in "that's not the most important thing to focus on." As in "have it or don't have it—either way, you'll still be left wanting."

I can promise you that you are not the center of the universe. I can promise you that I am not either. I am a sinner. So are you. So are your friends and neighbors. So are your spouse, your parents, your doctor, and your pastor.

There's good news in that, though. God is at work in the lives of sinners. In fact, the entire Bible is a narrative of God's redemptive plan for his people. If we rested in that fact, we would be fine. But it's easy not to just rest in that. It is easy to get nervous about giving up control, to be wary of trusting God's plan and allowing Him to do His thing in His way and His time. It isn't easy to believe that we are meant for greatness just because the Bible says so. We don't see the grand design as only God can, so we trust in what we know. But faith isn't about knowing. That's where doubt comes in: what we can see is harder to doubt. Jesus, having risen from the dead, said to Thomas, famously nicknamed doubting Thomas, "Because you have seen me, you have believed; blessed are those who have not seen and yet have believed" (John 20:29 NIV). Thomas actually saw the risen Christ; we have only words on pages. They may be the very word of God, but they are still words on pages. And it's a big, big book. A book that we are called to study both individually and as a community of faith. A book whose teachings we are called to learn and emulate. A book that is hard to take in without lots of help, so we look to people whose job it is to know, and we trust them.

Read that last sentence again. If you don't know any better—meaning, you haven't studied on your own—you might assume that whoever is standing on stage on Sunday morning knows what they're talking about. And if your pastor is gospel-centered, then you're all set. But if they aren't, and you don't have a foundation of your own apart from them, when they start saying things that aren't true, you're in a bad way and could start to take it in faith as God's Word.

Once I've clarified the existence of this disease of false teaching, my hope and prayer for you, the reader, is that you'll be equipped to recognize the differences—things like the call to give more to the church in order to get more from God, the claim that you can "name it and claim it" as yours from God by declaring what you want, the idea that you can't be sick or get hurt or die because of your faith, or that God wants you to be rich financially and without hardship. I want you to be strong enough to see those things and know them as false teachings and to stay true to the path of true faith—true to the understanding that He does want what's best for us, only we don't get to decide what "best" is. That is His job, and He does it well, even if we are too blind to see it. We are so blind, in fact, that many wander right past the atoning work of salvation in Christ and right into the mindset that God will shower you in gifts and keep you 100 percent healthy if only you do X, Y, or Z.

> *Father, I pray that you would open the heart of those who read these words. That you would fill them with your Holy Spirit and that they would be turned away from the false teachings of this world and pointed to you and the glory found in the image of your Son, Jesus. And I ask, Father, that your truth be spoken here, that it overshadow anything I would be tempted to say on my own and that through it all, it is You that gets the glory. May we each be changed today to reflect You and to look more like your Son, Jesus, and less like our sinful selves. I'm grateful to you, Father, in all things, and it is in your name I pray, amen.*

Think about it

1. Are you the main character in your story, with Christ as your best supporting actor? How's that working out for you? If Christ is the main character in your story, how did you make that shift?

2. When you go to church, read a book, or listen to a podcast that is teaching about God, how often do you accept it at face

value instead of thinking deeply about it and taking it back to the Bible? Do you think you would get more out of the lesson from researching what you read/heard in the Bible?

3. The Bible is a big book that's difficult to digest. What are your favorite ways to help dissect it and gain a deeper understanding of God's purpose for your life?

4. How often to you try to put into practice what you hear your pastor say? What damage could preaching a false gospel cause?

5. As you begin this book, what does prosperity specifically mean to you? When you think about God's "plans to prosper you" (Jeremiah 29:11), what does that look like for your life?

2

True Self-Help

Before I had Christ in my life, I was fairly successful. I was a hairdresser, technically I was an artistic educator and platform artist for a hair color and product company. What that means is that I traveled the country, sometimes even other countries, did hair for magazines and T.V., I did hair for models on the runway at fashion shows and hair conventions and taught other hairdressers how to better their skills. I won awards for it and had built quite a little name for myself, and it all looked really cool. But it wasn't.

The hair industry at that level is awful. Cutthroat, mean-spirited, sinful. Don't get me wrong: there are wonderful people too. I definitely don't mean to insult an entire industry of people in only the second chapter of the book. A few particular people were my sanity through it all and stood up for me when so many others didn't. And generally most hairdressers I met in salons as I traveled were great. But my larger experience in the business as a whole was confrontational and tremendously stressful. I fell further and further into the proverbial "den of vipers," and it was not all that long into the career that I became very me-focused. And once you make yourself the main character, it is hard to see beyond it. You start making choices that are subtly more selfish as the days, months, and years go on.

By the time I realized what was happening to me, it was too late. My family was still living together, but we were strangers. My marriage was nearly nonexistent. I didn't even know my children anymore. God forced me out of the hair industry through a carefully placed rear-end car accident that made it too hard on my back to stand for eight hours in a salon, and too hard on my entire body to sit for eight hours on a plane. As I mentioned at the opening of this chapter, I did a variety of things in the industry and those things were scattered all over the map so I traveled a lot. At least I did before the accident. So with the back problem likely to not end any time soon, I left hair. But what I learned through my career on stage teaching and performing in the hair industry was that I have a passion for teaching. A passion for leading. And a desire to help and inspire people.

So after reading a ton of self-help books, I came to the conclusion that I should tell the story of how being positive can drastically alter your destiny. It was what I believed as a hairdresser, and since I was a writer without any book in the works, that was as solid a plan as any. I set to work writing a book, writing a blog, developing a presentation, coming up with a niche to fit into, and trying to book gigs.

The funny thing was, being positive was not my strong suit. I wasn't already implementing what I was teaching and seeing a 180-degree change in my life. Things were not cupcakes and rainbows. Things were not positive. I was saying the right things and trying to believe that if I said it enough times it would become true. Without even knowing it, I was preaching the prosperity gospel.

It was a few months into that new life plan that things fell to the lowest low they had ever been. A second collision happened. The car I borrowed money for was a death trap, and we had to ditch it. Our debt was crippling. Our relationship was still there, but not really. The self-help books had helped, but I was still focused on myself. Even though I paid more attention to my wife and my kids, I was still the center. I was still the reason for everything. I was still thinking that I was the main character. Consequently, though I regularly told people that my dream was to change the world with my story, I was completely unable to change even my own world.

It didn't make sense. I did everything the books had described. And then, sitting on my kitchen counter, alone in the quiet hours of the night, I met Jesus.

It was Tuesday, December 26, 2017—the day when the course of my life radically began to shift. It was the day Jesus became not just a name I knew or a God I knew other people worshipped. It was the day He became real to me. I didn't know how exactly He was going to change me, but I knew that He was. Perhaps He already had. And when I say that, please know that I did not suddenly in that moment jump up and go, "Wow, Jesus, I give my life to you! I'm a changed man." No, it was subtle, but it was real. And now I had to test it.

I realized that I was not going to be able to do this on my own. And though my entire life was spent running from religion to religion, I had never even begun to consider a relationship with Him. This was the moment. I knew that I had to try Christianity. I was going to go to church. I would go, and then I'd know that it was just another wrong turn, like all the books were, like all the times before when I tried a new thing. At least then I could say I'd tried everything. I was expecting to listen to some guy talk about God for thirty minutes, hear a few songs I didn't know, and then head home wondering what to do next.

What happened was that God showed up.

It changed everything. The sermon was written as if I were the only person in the room. It hit me like a ton of bricks. Jesus, right there in that room of some six hundred people, met me face to face. And I was changed. I didn't officially give my heart to Him for several more months, but He had my heart my whole life—I just didn't know it. That's how God is with His people. That's when I began to realize that I—just like you, my friends—was not the main character. He was. He is. He always will be.

The prosperity gospel is attractive for one very pointed reason: it allows you to enjoy the love of God without the surrender that He requires of you. Prosperity gospel preachers will tell you that if you give enough to the church, and if you pray enough, God will give you everything you've ever wanted. And that simply isn't true. God will provide for you, yes. He will care for you 100 percent. He knows what you need, and He will see to it that you have it.

> It is written: Man shall not live on bread alone, but
> on every word that comes from the mouth of God.
> (Matthew 4:4 NIV)

Bread, in case you aren't familiar with the theological concept of this delicious, carby item, is referenced throughout scripture to represent one big concept, the things of this world that we need to live or more generally the provision of God. Usually, God provides the bread. In Exodus 16, God literally makes it rain manna, a breadlike item that fully sustained the Israelites every day. But the Israelites throughout the generations came to look at the *sustenance* as the thing they needed rather than God—just as we today focus too much on the gifts themselves, saying that the gifts represent God's love for us, or that unless we get the things we "need," God isn't for us. So we link the two things because if each of us is the main character, we must have an obedient God who rewards us.

Jesus knocks that idea right out in the passage from Matthew 4 above. I know it sounds great to keep getting the manna. Getting the stuff you want out of life sounds absolutely awesome. But my friends, the Lord is not our co-pilot—he *is* the pilot, and we are only passengers. We are not the pilot; we are not even the co-pilot. We are simply on the flight. We need to trust in Him. We survive on His provision, direction, and guidance, and surrendering to Him is the only way.

I told you that I was telling people I wanted to change the world with my story. But after that day in church, I realized that while I might very well get to change the world with a story, it's not going to be mine—it's going to be His. I only get to do the good works that He's prepared in advance for me to do (Ephesians 2:10). He prepared works for each of us in His story of redemption, a story about how He wants us back and sent His only Son to die for us so that we can be reconciled to Him.

1 Timothy 6:17–19 tells us:

> Command those who are rich in this present world
> not to be arrogant nor to put their hope in wealth,
> which is so uncertain, but to put their hope in God,
> who richly provides us with everything for our
> enjoyment. Command them to do good, to be rich in

good deeds, and to be generous and willing to share. In this way they will lay up treasure for themselves as a firm foundation for the coming age, so that they may take hold of the life that is truly life.

God has a rich life prepared for you. A life that is truly living. A life full of enjoyment and generosity. I say it's time to embrace it—not so that you get what you want, but because a life with Christ is the only thing worth wanting. And when you have it, everything else is icing on the cake.

Think about it

1. Has your life ever changed direction dramatically? Afterwards, were you able to see God's hand in the change? How did you feel at the time in comparison to how you feel about that change now?

2. What blessings have you received over the course of your life? Do you find it easier to worship the blessings than the Giver of those blessings? Why do you think that is?

3. What does a "life worth truly living" look like to you?

4. In light of Matthew 4:4, how would you say that God providing is for you through His Word?

5. Do you think God loves you but can still make things hard? Or that God will give you provision you didn't want or weren't expecting?

What Is Prosperity Gospel, Anyway?

There are many ways to define "prosperity gospel." For purposes of this book, I define "prosperity gospel" as a controversial religious belief among some Protestant Christians who hold that financial blessing and physical well-being are always the will of God for them, and that faith, positive speech, and donations to religious causes will increase one's material wealth.

Prosperity theology regards the Bible as a contract between God and humans. If humans have faith in God, He will deliver security and prosperity. The doctrine emphasizes the importance of personal empowerment, proposing that it is God's will for His people to be blessed. The atonement, or reconciliation with God, is interpreted to include the alleviation of sickness and poverty, which are viewed as curses to be broken by faith, believed to be achieved through donations of money, visualization, and positive confession.

Sounds great, right? It's as if we are saying "We believe in God, God loves us unconditionally, and therefore He must want what we want: to have top-notch financial and physical standing. I mean, just look at John 3:16: *For God so loved the world that He gave His one and only Son, that whoever believes in Him shall not perish but have eternal life* If He is going to send His only Son, one of the three persons of the Trinity, to die a miserable death on a cross, then surely He must want the best for us." But that isn't at all what the gospel tells us. The good news of Jesus Christ isn't that life is going to be cupcakes and rainbows now.

Stephen Hunt, professor of sociology at the University of the West of England, explains prosperity gospel this way:

> In the forefront is the doctrine of the assurance of "divine" physical health and prosperity through faith. In short, this means that "health and wealth" are the automatic divine right of all Bible-believing Christians and may be procreated by faith as part of the package of salvation.

The reality is this: you can take any words you like and change them to mean whatever you want. Taken out of context, the Bible can deliver nearly any message you want. This is what we call *eisegesis*, the opposite of exegesis. Dictionary.com defines *eisegesis* as "an interpretation, especially of Scripture, that expresses the interpreter's own ideas, bias, or the like, rather than the meaning of the text." So you see how it can easily become a breeding ground for false teachings when we read into scripture what *we* want to rather than seeing what it's truly saying.

It is happening more and more frequently that a megachurch will spring up, bring thousands of people to Christ, and make big waves. Let's celebrate that 100 percent. But if those new Christians—"baby Christians" as it were—aren't really taught the gospel, then how are they to live out their faith? The vision of the megachurch often is to "seek and save the lost" but typically is not focused on education and Bible teaching, so the new Christian is left to try to figure out what it all means. Then at the slightest bump to their faith, they lose it because they were never taught the fundamentals. If the church is doing its job—any church, not just the big ones—it is both reaching out to lost people to bring them in and teaching those who are in the building how to live out their faith through a life lived with and for Christ using the Word of God. In saying that, I acknowledge that not all megachurches are establishments for preaching prosperity gospel. It is just very common. The little backwoods church in the middle of Nowheresville might do the same thing. And I'm not anti-megachurch any more than I am anti-little church. I am just anti-false gospel.

To put it different way, how can you talk about a movie accurately if you've only seen the trailer? So it is with these untaught Christians, left to learn on their own. And some of them certainly do. But it is the exception, not the rule, that finds people teaching themselves the gospel without guidance or encouragement. That's why Jesus commanded us in Matthew 28 to go and make disciples, because discipling someone takes relationship, intentionality, and a desire to pass on the faith.

So when a prosperity gospel preacher tells the congregation that if they give to the church, they are showing their faith and God wants to reward them for it, people don't know any better than to eat it up. People are hungry, desperately wanting better than they have—sometimes out of the need for better, other times out of greed, lust, and selfishness. But whatever the reason, it is our nature to want more. That's where phrases like "go big or go home" come from. That's why even though there are six drink sizes to choose from at the drive-through, the two biggest sellers are the smallest size, because it comes in a kid's meal, and the largest size, because we want more.

And if our mindset is "more is better," and we think of ourselves as the main character in the story of our lives, then it stands to reason that the role of God in our story would be to want what's best for us. If we have to pay the church to show God our faith and thus to get the wealth and health we want, then why not do it? Seems easy enough, right? And so it goes for an increasingly large number of people.

The problem is, it isn't our story. It's God's. So many times the attendees of prosperity-preaching churches don't get the wealth their pastor promised them, or they get sick, or their family gets sick or hurt. Then what?

I'll tell you what: those people question God. Since they are the main character in their story, they can't be in the wrong, so it must be God. But the Gospel, the real Gospel, doesn't promise health and wealth. It promises that no matter how hard life gets—and it will get hard—Christ is with you through it. It teaches us that we don't have to be afraid of life's hardships when Christ has given us the gift of eternal life and we need not live in fear: "Even though I walk through the valley of the shadow of death, I will fear no evil, for you are with me" (Psalm 23:4a ESV).

One further point about prosperity gospel that is possibly the most frustrating part for me. Those among us who are most likely to fall into the false teachings of prosperity gospel are the underprivileged, the lower-income, the lesser educated. Remember,

Jesus came first to the poor, the sick, the destitute. The wealthy typically didn't end up on the warm and fuzzy end of His ministry. If Christ came for the poor, the sick, and the needy, then I guess with the right wording you can make it seem that prosperity theology lines up perfectly with the mission of Christ Himself. On closer inspection, it's exploitative of their situation to pull the wool over their eyes. The reality is that Jesus didn't say they would believe in Him and suddenly everything would get better. On the contrary, in the Sermon on the Mount (Matthew 5–7), Jesus speaks of the persecuted, the meek, and the poor in spirit, and how they are blessed. And those blessings are not wealth or health. At the close of the Beatitudes, we as Christians are told clearly how we will be blessed: "Rejoice and be glad, for your reward is great in heaven, for so they persecuted the prophets who were before you" (Matthew 5:12 ESV).

Lots to be happy about, but not in the immediate present and maybe not even on this Earth. If we are rejoicing in our present rewards, we are not really putting our faith and trust in God. Pastor and author John Piper said it this way: "Prosperity cannot be proof of God's favor for this is what the Devil promises to those who worship him." He's referring to Matthew 4:8–9: "Again, the devil took him to a very high mountain and showed him all the kingdoms of the world and their splendor. 'All this I will give you,' he said, 'if you will bow down and worship me'" (NIV).

The rubber meets the road in this shift in your understanding. You see, if we are looking at our budget, we should see God in our circumstances whether wealthy or impoverished. If we are looking at our health, we should see God at work in a clean bill of health, the perfectly fit body that cuts every curve in just the right way, but also in the cancer diagnosis, the extra pounds we can't seem to lose, and the depression. If we are looking at our family life, we have to see Him in the happy marriage and the broken one, the house full of kids and the house without kids. We have to see Him in parents who love us and in parents who don't. God is present in all circumstances, and He loves us in all circumstances.

Think about it

1. What is your impression of prosperity gospel as defined here? Do you agree, or disagree? Why?

2. What is your definition of "what's best for us"? What is God's definition of that same phrase? How are they different?

3. Have you ever participated in eisegesis? Have you ever gone to the Word for an answer and picked out what you wanted to hear from it, rather than listening for God's direction?

4. Seeing prosperity in the good and the bad is a difficult concept. How are you able to tackle this idea, and what makes it easier to find the manna from heaven even in the tough times?

4

The One True Gospel

The word *gospel* means "good news." When you hear Christians referring to the Good News of Jesus Christ, they mean the Gospel. I've come to realize, though, that there are a good many Christians who are either uncomfortable with or unable to articulate what that good news is, outside of saying something superficial like "Jesus saves"—which, while totally accurate, doesn't explain anything. I don't think it's their fault, or not entirely. And if I've just described you to some extent, that's OK. American church culture of the twenty-first century is less educational and more experiential than church has ever been. I am by no means against a moving experience during a worship service. I love a good electric guitar, some haze, and a great light show. But I don't go to church to see that. I go for the message. I go to hear the Word of God preached.

I've heard several charismatic preachers say that they are out to seek and save the lost. That their goal is to bring in as many people to their church as possible to hear the Word, and that they aspire to train others to do the same. The intention to reach lost sheep is awesome as a starting point, but not as a resting point. You have got to teach your congregation *how* to reach those lost sheep. And it is not by hyping up the experience of your church service. Not by adding more lights, more effects, more instruments or theatrics. You can go down that road to get them in—be like the world to attract the world. But once they are in the seats, hit them with sound gospel teaching. It is through the gospel shared from stages and through intentional, individual relationships that the world gets changed. And certainly some very large churches do both the big show and small group study. But that is the exception to what normally happens, not the rule.

The apostle Paul writes, "these things which you have heard me say in the presence of many witnesses, entrust to reliable people who will be qualified to teach others" (2 Timothy 2:2 NIV). He is speaking of the gospel of Jesus and how we should be teaching it to people and in turn teaching them to teach it to others. My pastor calls it spiritual multiplication. And if you don't think you can do it, then this chapter is the most important one in this entire book.

I have what I believe is an easy way to understand and share the gospel, and it is simply these four words:

Creation
Corruption
Crucifixion
Construction

These are the bones on which you can build the flesh of the Bible. There are many other ways to break it down, so if you have heard the gospel already and these aren't the exact words you use, remember this: if God had meant for His Word to be easily taught in a few words, the Bible would contain only a few words. Don't get caught up in the minutia of complicated stories in scripture. Begin with simple study of the characters, the major events, and the person and work of Christ. All the little details that are weird to understand can add to your understanding later on in your spiritual walk.

Creation

Let's begin with, well, the beginning: the account of Genesis 1 and 2, the beginning of our world, the story of how it all came to be. The Bible is written in many literary modes: history, genealogy, poetry, parables, and more. Many people read Genesis 1 as historical narrative, therefore to be taken literally. Others place it in the tradition of Hebrew poetry. I am of the camp that sees it very much as historical drama. Nobody was there to watch it happen, but the original language as I've understood it tells the story of why, more than it does how, God created everything. Therefore we can look back and have healthy discussion about things like space, time, cosmology, dinosaurs, etc with other Christians without anyone being truly wrong or right. Perhaps even in saying that I've made Genesis more confusing and I'm sorry for that. Language barriers and the problems of translation also have to be taken into consideration. These are important questions, and what this all means for you and me is that Genesis might not be written to be taken literally. But the confusion these questions generate among people who explore the minutiae should cause us to take a step back and ask what really matters. The important part is simply this: *In the beginning, God.*

Moses wrote the Torah, which comprises the five books that begin the Bible, and he most definitely was not alive to watch Creation for himself. So wherever you find yourself in the argument regarding Creation, I think, or at least I venture to hope, that we can all agree that God was revealing the deep love by which He endeavored to create our world. He made it perfectly, and He gave us dominion over it. We were made in His image, an image that is love poured out. And when we ate the fruit of the tree of the knowledge of good and evil (Genesis 3:6), whether you take that to be literal or figurative, sin entered the world and we lost our perfection—and in so doing, we lost our union with God. Even though the Creation story is only two chapters of the first book of the Bible, and there are sixty-six books in total, it is extremely important to begin with Creation when teaching the gospel. If you don't know what the world was originally created to be like, and what it eventually will be again, then you have no reason to believe anything else.

Corruption

It all falls apart in Genesis 3. We did the one thing God had commanded us not to do, and we immediately knew we messed up. Adam and Eve hid from God because they knew what they'd done. They felt shame. They felt guilt:

> Then the man and his wife heard the sound of the Lord God as he was walking in the garden in the cool of the day, and they hid from the Lord God among the trees of the garden. But the Lord God called to the

man, 'Where are you?' He answered, 'I heard you in the garden, and I was afraid because I was naked; so I hid.' And he said, 'Who told you that you were naked? Have you eaten from the tree that I commanded you not to eat from?' The man said, 'The woman you put here with me—she gave me some fruit from the tree, and I ate it.' Then the Lord God said to the woman, 'What is this you have done?' The woman said, 'The serpent deceived me, and I ate.' ... The Lord God made garments of skin for Adam and his wife and clothed them." (Genesis 3:8-13, 21 NIV)

Sin entered the world, entered us as people, and it has been getting exponentially worse ever since. They ate fruit, their offspring murdered. A few generations later there was mass murder and adultery. It's all there in black and white, and sometimes red (at least in the New Testament). Fast forward many hundreds of generations, and you end up here with us, twenty-first-century humanity, ripe with sin of all shapes and sizes. So steeped with sin that we can't see past it at all. The sixteenth-century Swiss reformer John Calvin called it "total depravity." American theologian and pastor R. C. Sproul called it "radical corruption." However you describe it, the reality is clear. We are, through and through, sinners: "Every inclination of the thoughts of the human heart are only evil all the time" (Genesis 6:5 NIV). I like how the New Living Translation says it too: "The Lord observed the extent of human wickedness on the earth, and he saw that everything they thought or imagined was consistently and totally evil." That means that no matter how hard we try, we are simply not fixing this mess on our own. Even our attempts to fix the problem are perpetuating the problem.

Crucifixion

He told us what would happen, we didn't listen, and He did exactly what He said He would. God told us that disobedience to Him (sinning) would equal death. But if you're thinking, "when He gave that warning to Adam, He said Adam would die, and Adam and Eve didn't die." You're right, He said the punishment is death. Read the passage from Genesis again. Do you see it? Do you see the punishment carried out? Let me explain.

They were hiding, riddled with shame. What did God do? He gave them garments. Where did those skins come from? Animals. And can an animal live without skin? No. So did He punish with death? He did. That means that those animals died in place of Adam and Eve to cover over the bodies of the now sinful humans. He sacrificed the animals to literally cover up our sin. This is the first time you see the Crucifixion foreshadowed in scripture. We say Jesus atoned for our sins. The word atone that we use to explain Jesus satisfying the punishment we earned before God comes from a Hebrew word כָּפַר (*kaphar*) which literally means to cover over. God covered our bodies then through the sacrifice He made of those animals. So when people tell you that the Old Testament and the New Testament are separate bibles, you can chuckle to yourself and then softly explain Genesis 3:21.

The thing to remember is that the punishment for sin is death. And because everyone sins, we all deserve punishment. And if God doesn't deliver His punishment, He isn't a just God. He describes himself as just, so if He didn't exact punishment where it is earned, He would be contradicting Himself and would thus not be God.

But He loved us so much that He took on his own punishment. He did the thing we were unable to do. He came to earth as a man:

"And the Word was made flesh, and dwelt among us" (John 1:14a KJV). He lived a perfect life. He went to the cross and died the death *we* deserved. We are saved by Him, not through ourselves or our efforts. Our salvation is from God. He took on our sin, and in its place gave us His righteousness. The big churchy explanation is "double imputation". We imputed our sin to Him, and He imputed His righteousness to us. And we are now free to live a life with and for Him.

Construction

What does it mean to live a life with and for Him? It means that we are called by Him to do what He has for us to do, His plan, His purpose: "And we know that in all things God works for the good of those who love him, who have been called according to his purpose" (Romans 8:28 NIV). We have the opportunity, the blessing, the joy of being part of His story—to build the kingdom He promised us. We get to live as He lived, love as He loved, and spread the message of His gospel so that others can do the same.

The Spirit is building within each of us the qualities of Christ that we were always meant to have. The love we pour out will help build up other people and fight back the destructive force that is the world around us. We build communities of believers who support and build up one another.

When I teach people the four Cs, I get the most push back on the concept of construction. I hope I've written the word "build" enough times to help it make sense. And if anyone ever tells you they believe in the big bang theory, tell them that you do too, because C-4 is explosive.

Think about it

1. Do you have difficulty sharing the gospel? If so, why? If not, how do you tell people about it?

2. Did you learn a way to share the gospel that differs from the four Cs? If so, what is it? If not, was the 4 C's new to you? Do you think you could see yourself telling them to someone today? Why or why not?

3. Did you know Jesus was foreshadowed so early in the Bible? What do you think of that?

4. Have you ever tried to fix something but just made it worse? How do you see this happening as a result of corruption throughout the Bible and into the present?

5. How can you live a life with Him and for him?

5

Does God Desire
Our Prosperity?

In the epistle to the Romans, Paul gives the church in Rome a clear vision of God's desire for our prosperity:

> May the God of hope fill you with all joy and peace
> as you trust in him, so that you may overflow with
> hope by the power of the Holy Spirit. (Romans
> 15:13 NIV)

But if you listen closely to what Paul is saying, it's not that He wants us to be full of joy in our stuff, or that He wants us to overflow with hope in the receiving of even more than we have or in the excitement over gaining more. Prosperity gospel, as we've seen, affirms that God wants us to have stuff—in fact, that by prayer and good will, we actually *deserve* prosperity. I'm not an expert in theology, nor would I say that my knowledge of scripture makes me an expert. I will say, though, that it's hard to miss what Paul's words are driving at: "as you trust in Him." The English Standard Version translates that same passage above in Romans as "in believing." This is not a "manifest your best life by the power of positive thinking" type of sentiment. This is God giving you what you *need*, not necessarily what you want, when you believe in Him. And when you come to know Him, there isn't anything more you need, which means you have everything. And from a prosperity standpoint, having everything would mean you're prospering.

John, the disciple whom Jesus loved, writes in his gospel what God desires for us, and how what He desires sits in contrast to the rest of the world.

"The thief comes only to steal and kill and destroy; I have come that they may have life, and have it to the full." (John 10:10)

If we think about what Jesus is saying here, the fullness of life is not a fountain of stuff, yet most prosperity gospel preachers will point to this passage to support their doctrine. Typically you'll hear it preached from the pulpit without the first half, making it easier to change the meaning. His teaching here is meant as a comparison between a life lived with the world, constantly in conflict with those around you and in conflict with the way it was always supposed to be. The sin in our hearts steals away our righteousness. That sin kills us, leaving us unto death and destroying all that God made perfect. Yet He comes that we may have life, no longer dead in our sin. He defeated sin and death on a hill called Calvary, and in so doing, purchased for us a salvation we could never afford on our own. The fullness of a life in Christ is to have a life lived with and for Him, as it was supposed to be in Genesis 1 and 2, before the Fall.

But what we bring to the passage, eisegesis, makes it feel like a promise from Christ to give us a full life on our terms—we believe in Him and get what we feel would make our lives full. In fact, Jesus never says anything about us setting our own terms. If we were to make a list of our wants and in essence tell God what would make us "full," we would be positioning ourselves above Him and reducing Him to a divine Amazon Prime membership.

Maybe that sounds a bit ludicrous, it was meant to, but that is what you're truly saying. It's a proclamation that your wants and needs are paramount, and God, in exchange for your belief in and prayers to Him, should do what you want. You pay the fee (prayer) and you get the product (prosperity), like buying a smart device for your life: "Alexa, give me a really nice car, a bigger house, and a fully loaded checking account."

That makes perfect sense if we are the main character. Why not have a genie or something that gives us what we want? It's no fun for the main character to obey the will of another character. But the fact of the matter is that we aren't called to manifest our dream life or to will what we want into being. We're called to follow Christ. You see that in Christ's words to his disciples:

> Then Jesus told his disciples, "If anyone would come after me, let him deny himself and take up his cross and follow me. For whoever would save his life will lose it, but whoever loses his life for my sake will find it. For what will it profit a man if he gains the whole

world and forfeits his soul? Or what shall a man give
in return for his soul?" (Matthew 16:24–26 ESV)

We are in a beautiful novel, an incredible story in which our
lives are elegantly written about in explicit detail. But we are not the
main character. We follow the main character. We deny ourselves
the things we think we want and we think are best for us. We take
up our cross, the sin we carry (our struggles, faults, pains, mistakes),
and follow His lead.

Jesus states unequivocally that whoever would save his life will
lose it. If you take the perspective that you are the main character,
it would make sense that you would do all you can to keep yourself
on top—to "save" your life. But if you work super-duper hard to
save yourself, you might live with cool stuff for a little while, but
ultimately, you can't take it with you. Even if you lived longer
than anyone ever, you will ultimately leave all of it behind. The
oldest person whose age has been independently verified was
Jeanne Calment (1875–1997) of France, who lived to the age of
122 years—164 days, and she still left her body and all of her
things behind at her death. With an average lifespan of seventy-
one years—or even if you live longer than Jeanne, who outdid
the average by more than fifty years—you still keep the stuff you
worked for so hard for only so long.

If you lose your life of self-sufficiency—or I would posit, self-
insufficiency—you will gain eternal life in Christ. He even lands the
plane by asking rhetorically, "For what will it profit a man if he gains
the whole world and forfeits his soul?" He doesn't need you to answer;
the answer is clear just by doing the math: around seventy-one years,
maybe as long as 122 years or so, on earth with your earthly treasures

versus infinite years in heaven living in sinless perfection. I'm not even a little good in math, but this equation is a no-brainer.

The math problem is articulated even more clearly in the best-selling novel *Jesus + Nothing = Everything* by pastor and author Tullian Tchividjian, grandson of the well-known evangelist Billy Graham, who wrote this regarding how we ought to live our lives:

> Daily Christian living, in other words, is daily Christian dying: Dying to our trivial comforts, soul-shrinking conveniences, arrogant preferences, and self-centered entitlements, and living for something much larger than what makes us comfortable and safe.

And still we love, love, love stuff. We love saying we own stuff, talking about owning stuff, planning out more stuff to own—and if it isn't stuff, its status. Wanting it, gaining it, having it. But none of it does any long-term good to help us feel full. Businessman and millionaire John D. Rockefeller was once asked how much money was enough, to which he famously replied, "Just a little more." The man had more money than the governments of some countries, and even in that he wasn't content. But his reply tells something even deeper. Not only did he acknowledge that he wasn't happy, but his ambiguous answer shows how truly undefined and ultimately unreachable his happiness was. A little more than what?

To quote the twentieth-century philosopher Christopher Wallace, aka Biggie Smalls, in his work *Mo Money Mo Problems*, "It's like the more money we come across, the more problems we see." If you can learn anything from the 1990s rap scene, it's that. The bigger your bank account, the larger your problems become. And for some reason we keep wanting more. The Bible's teachings on money confirm that struggle (see 1 Timothy 6:10) because it is very real, and God tells us in His Word that He will be the one to sustain us, not our money or the problems we find ourselves having because of it. He calls us to set those problems down and follow Him instead (Psalm 55:22).

We can certainly believe that our story is important, because it is. But you don't need to be the main character to be important, to have purpose. Yoda is considered an ancillary character; Albus Dumbledore isn't the main character either, nor are Splinter, Morpheus, the Mad Hatter, the Tin Man, the Pink Ladies, and Marla Singer. But they were each valuable to the story and important to the main character. (And if any of those characters didn't ring a bell, google them immediately and watch them in action.)

In the same way, we are all part of God's story, but it is most certainly His story. God uses everything that goes on in the lives of everyone in the past, present, and future for His glory. Our prosperity is something he desires for us. But He, being omniscient, knows what prosperity truly means. Eternity in His presence is how I define prosperity, and I hope you will see that you should as well.

Think about it:

1. When you imagined God as an Amazon Prime membership, how did that make you feel? Do you think you could ever be fulfilled if that were real?

2. How would you define the fullness of life?

3. How do you feel about being a secondary character? Does that give you peace that you aren't in control, or make you feel anxious that you aren't in control?

4. As you read through this book, how is your definition of prosperity changing?

Good Intentions versus Intentional Living

The falseness of prosperity gospel arises from the reworking that it does of how we should understand our path. Jesus says,

> "Enter through the narrow gate. For wide is the gate and broad is the road that leads to destruction, and many enter through it. But small is the gate and narrow the road that leads to life, and only a few find it." (Matthew 7:13–14 NIV)

Interestingly enough, the very next verse is a warning about false teachers who will tell you that the path is much easier: "Watch out for false prophets. They come to you in sheep's clothing, but inwardly they are ferocious wolves" (Matthew 7:15 NIV). Remember that false teachers don't benefit from being so fanatical that they are not followed. So they will twist the truth just a little bit—take a Bible verse out of context, for example, and use it to achieve an end other than the Lord intended.

They say the road to hell is paved with good intentions. Jesus's words in the passage from Matthew make that obvious. But to get deeper into the reasons why good intentions are the pavement of that road, we should first distinguish between intentional living and good intentions.

Good intentions form the general state of desiring something for a "good" reason. I might even say that good intentions are the sentiment of wanting. We never want anything for a bad reason, right? Even if you go down the road of thinking about the bad things we may want—for example, you want to hurt someone because they hurt you first—your *good* intention is to defend yourself. You aren't thinking, "Man, I wish I could be a worse person than I am and just beat that person up." You're thinking, "Man, I don't deserve this, and I'm going to defend myself." Or what about people who starve themselves into anorexia. They aren't thinking, "You know what I really need? An eating disorder." They want to look and feel better. It is a good intention.

There was a time in my own life when my marriage was in the dirt, and although the best thing I could have done for myself was to be home more and focus on my family, what I did was spend more time at work. This was during the time I was a hairdresser, and O just kept booking clients earlier in the day and later in the day to make my shifts longer. I wasn't thinking, "Oh wow, I can't wait to see how much distance I can create between my wife and me." I would say to myself, "The extra money this will bring will make life easier."

Intentional living, on the other hand, involves thinking about our actions, focusing on the day and doing life on purpose. I've heard people say it's like living life on fire. More specifically, that purpose is the Lord. We live for the glory of God. He is the one who holds the cards. He calls us into a life of intention, a life of purpose. The building of His kingdom is the purpose, and it is so cool that the God of the universe chose us to participate in this purpose.

Therein lies the problem, though. Søren Kierkegaard said in *Sickness unto Death*, "It is the normal state of the human heart to try to build its identity around something besides God." Since it is God's purpose that we align ourselves with Him, but our heart's normal state is to identify ourselves as other than God, we are in opposition to God right from the jump. The irony is that we are made in the image of God, and so we should be up to the task of following His lead. But Jeremiah 17:9 says, "The heart is deceitful above all things, and desperately sick; who can understand it?" And Genesis 6:5 (NIV) says, "every inclination of the thoughts of the human heart is all evil all the time."

We work hard to follow the goals we set for ourselves. But when our heart is oriented towards our own self-interests, the intention is misdirected. Paul tells of what happens when our heart is in the driver's seat:

> The acts of the flesh are obvious: sexual immorality, impurity and debauchery; idolatry and witchcraft; hatred, discord, jealousy, fits of rage, selfish ambition, dissensions, factions and envy; drunkenness, orgies, and the like. I warn you, as I did before, that those who live like this will not inherit the kingdom of

God. But the fruit of the Spirit is love, joy, peace, forbearance, kindness, goodness, faithfulness, gentleness and self-control. Against such things there is no law. Those who belong to Christ Jesus have crucified the flesh with its passions and desires. Since we live by the Spirit, let us keep in step with the Spirit. (Galatians 5:19–25 NIV)

You can see clearly that there is an opposition between the two ways of living. Living in step with the flesh is by far the easier route. And we would say of those choices that they began with good intentions. Does anybody make sinful choices with the intention of being sinful? But when asked why we did something, we respond with "no reason." The truth is, we didn't do it for no reason. Of course there's a reason—just not a good one. The reason may be a bad or inappropriate one. To put it a different way, we didn't do it because of the negative. We did it for the positive, the pleasure it brought us.

Let's look at just a few of Paul's examples—and be mindful that he was not writing an exhaustive list, so there are more fleshly acts that he could name, as indicated by the open-ended "and the like" tag at the end of the statement.

Paul begins with sexual immorality. Imagine a husband and wife whose relationship is broken by the husband's marital infidelity. The thoughts going through his head as he has sexual relations with a woman other than his wife are probably not "Man, I can't wait to ruin my marriage!" or "This STD is going to be amazing." And he certainly isn't picturing his crying children or the divorce attorney bills or the therapy that his wife may need afterwards. No, his thoughts are on the pleasure of his immediate actions—the pros of the choice, not the cons.

The same is true of every sin we commit. Take lying as an example not on Paul's list. The absence of an obvious sin like lying should be a clue that a list in scripture may not be complete but meant to give a framework of examples to lead you to your own conclusions. I think of it as leaving room to insert your own issues.

Lying is one of those things we as a culture have made ourselves OK with. We even have a cute little term for lies that are OK to tell. We call them "white lies," as if that makes them better. So I'm late getting home from work; if I tell my wife that there was an accident on the highway that slowed traffic to a standstill for an hour, that is a believable situation, and she says "OK, dinner's ready," and we move on with our night. But what if I'm late because I made a pit stop to have fun with my friends for a bit? It doesn't hurt her really, right? I told the lie so I wouldn't get into a fight. She isn't harmed, and life goes on. See what I mean? I make it about the "good" intention, not the "bad" lie.

And then when caught and asked why you lied, more often than not in my own life I would respond to a situation like the one above with an answer like "No reason." But the sarcastic retort "no reason" doesn't mean there is no reason; the real meaning could be that it was fun to do, and the person doing it didn't think it through all the way but just did it. Just for fun, for immediate gratification, without regard for the negative impact and instead only regarding the positive expected. I should be clear that you might still get "bad" results from doing the right or good thing. Like what happens when your wife says "Do these jeans make me look fat?" If they do, there has got to be a nicer way to respond than to simply say "yes" but either way you're likely to hurt her feelings.

What would truly intentional living look like? I would tell my wife that I was thinking of going out with some friends after work instead of coming home and ask whether she had any plans for the night that would be affected negatively. She might say, "Of course not. I'll make less for dinner, and you go out and eat with your friends. I love you." Then we're good. If she says, "I'd really like you home; I've had a tough day," then I would choose to skip the friends and come home. The choice would be based on honoring the Lord and the calling He has placed on my life to be a good and loving husband. It's about putting the needs of others before my own, whereas good intentions are often veiled in self-interest.

I hope that you are starting to see the difference between good intentions and an intentional life. To really understand the truth of God and His desire for your life, and to truly understand why you should not fall victim to the prosperity gospel, you need to be clear about the difference. Prosperity theology will tell you that if you live your best life, you can manifest whatever you want, that God will get in step with what you want for yourself. And there is plenty of good intention with that. But it's putting that cart before the horse.

That way of thinking tells you that if you do X, Y, and Z, then God will do whatever you want. Your "good" intention is to follow God's rules. The issue there is that it isn't how God is calling you to live; it's the expectation that He ought to do what you want. There aren't boxes for Christians to check off so that you do as you want with the Lord as your co-pilot. No, no: God is the pilot, and you follow His lead. Period.

Then what does it mean to live intentionally, if all we have are our so-called good intentions? Doesn't God tell us to give of ourself, to put the needs of others ahead of ourselves? Isn't that the nature of a servant, which Jesus tells us to be because He Himself came as (see Matthew 20:28 and Mark 10:25, compare John 13:1-17) He does, but not so we can stand confidently and ask for things. He wants us to acknowledge that all we have is from Him and that submission to His will involves trust and surrender.

Let's say you saw a young man helping an elderly woman carry her groceries across a busy street. How might you view his actions differently if you could hear his thoughts? "I'm so glad I was here to help her" would make you feel that he is a wonderful man. But his thought might be, "I just saw my boss standing over there, and I sure hope he sees me doing this so he thinks I'm a great person. Maybe that'll help me get the promotion." It's the same action from the same man, but wouldn't knowing his motivation cause you to consider him self-centered?

That is the difference between good intentions and intentional living. The Lord God tells us to be kind and loving to those in need, and often focuses on the widow, children, the sick. He wants us to care for those people because we are spiritually in need in the same way that they are physically in need. It is an exercise in loving our neighbor as ourselves, a practice of sacrificial love as He sacrificed for us.

If your pastor is telling you that you need to tithe so that God hears you or so that you may be healed, at best he has good intentions. But what he doesn't have is right teaching. The money you are giving is not part of an if-then transaction. The money you have is yours only because God willed it so. It is on loan to you from Him.

What if a friend handed you $20 when you were in need but then asked you to buy them a soda with it, saying you could keep the change? You wouldn't turn to them and say, "Sorry, money is tight, and I need the whole thing." I imagine that you would gratefully hold onto the remaining $18 after grabbing them the soda. So it is with God. It really isn't any more complicated than that. You have your health because God wills that you are currently healthy. Giving more to the church won't keep you healthy or make you healthier. Praying more won't either. Nor will it make you wealthier.

Be a good steward of the money He gives you, and if He wills it so, He will give you more: "Whoever can be trusted with very little can also be trusted with much, and whoever is dishonest with very little will also be dishonest with much" (Luke 16:10 NIV). So can He trust you with little? If your check is only $100, but we are called to tithe to the church the first 10 percent, that means that really you have $90 to spend. (See Malachi 3:10NIV and Leviticus 27:30-33ESV, compare Hebrews 7:1-28) Just as in my soda example, the friend is giving you $18, not $20. So do not fall into the trap of thinking that you can trade your tithe for God's obedience to your will. It doesn't happen that way. The Lord never once promises health, wealth, and happiness. The Israelites, as well as the early church of the New Testament, suffered much even though they were tithing and praying more than most of modern Christendom does today. We tithe, we pray, we serve because our God and Heavenly Father says to. Trust that His sovereign will is at work and will take care of your needs better than you can on your own.

That may sound like a tough pill to swallow, but I submit to you that Jesus is clear, and I love the way the Contemporary English Version puts it: "Look at the birds in the sky! They don't plant or

41

harvest. They don't even store grain in barns. Yet your Father in heaven takes care of them. Aren't you worth much more than birds?" (Matt. 6:26, CEV). If you live intentionally along the path God has for you, it is a sure thing that you will be taken care of. Remember that you are not immune from hardship, but you are well led and therefore you will make it through hardship.

Remember also that intentional living does not mean living without sin. Only Christ lived sinlessly, and we are not capable in our fallen state of following in those footsteps. Those What Would Jesus Do bracelets that were so popular a decade or two ago had good intentions but left a whole generation (my generation, actually) feeling insufficient. The real philosophy that Jesus espoused was to do what He said, not what He did. So instead we should ask ourselves, "What would Jesus *say* to do?" And to know that, we must read the Bible to find out. If that's a struggle for you, I get it, believe me. But there are tons of resources out there to help you get into God's Word more deeply. I happen to like BibleSteps.org and PROScritpure.com as starting points; they offer great tools to utilize in the quest to understand scripture better and spend more time with it.

I'm going to end this chapter with a fun realization I had while thinking through the idea of intentional living, or rather intentionally following God's will for my life. I realized, not for the first time but certainly with renewed clarity, that Christianity is not a religion of rules to be followed. It is a call into a relationship with a personal Lord and Savior. And with that two things came to light. First, the Lord desires our good: "And we know that in all things God works for the good of those who love him, who have been called according to his purpose" (Romans 8:28 NIV). And second, the Savior of the world intended for us to live positively and to stay positive. An aggressive posture is the opposite of helpful. Even as He was being arrested, Jesus was able to stay positive, and He rebuked Peter for being aggressive towards the guards. "'Put your sword back in its place,' Jesus said to him, 'for all who draw the sword will die by the sword'" (Matthew 26:52 NIV). And the apostle Paul reminds us in his first epistle to the church in Thessalonica to "rejoice always, pray continually, give thanks in all circumstances; for this is God's will for you in Christ Jesus" (1 Thessalonians 5:16–18 NIV).

The Word of God is clear on the subject of positivity. What it says is that to live in step with the Holy Spirit, or as I've been putting it, to live intentionally for Him, is to remain positive—to rejoice, pray, and be thankful.

Think about it

1. After reading this chapter, how can you define the difference between good intentions and intentional living in your own life?

2. What have you done in the past with good intentions? Were there consequences to your actions?

3. How can you live more intentionally today?

4. How does positivity play into intentionally living for you?

5. Do you think intentional living will help you prosper? In what way?

7

Leveraging Positivity

C. S. Lewis wrote to his friend, the American author Sheldon Vanauken, that "It is a Christian's duty, as you know, for everyone to be as happy as he can." It isn't a stretch for us to begin to see the idea that God desires us to be happy—and that our happiness can be, in fact must be, found in Him. Anything aside from Him that we ascribe our happiness to is fleeting and fleshly, only temporary, and will most certainly leave us with a feeling of wanting more. So if you are to focus attentively on the Spirit and God's will for your life, it is worth pursuing the notion of positivity. And how does one go about leveraging positivity, as this chapter's title so bluntly suggests doing?

The Bible is full of passages worth studying to gain wisdom for living with a bend towards positivity. Let's begin by looking at three.

Do not boast about tomorrow, for you do not
know what a day may bring. Let someone else
praise you, and not your own mouth; an outsider,
and not your own lips ... Anger is cruel and fury
overwhelming, but who can stand before jealousy?
(Proverbs 27:1–2, 4 NIV)

Whatever is true, whatever is honorable, whatever
is just, whatever is pure, whatever is lovely, whatever
is commendable, if there is any excellence, if there is
anything worthy of praise, think about these things."
(Philippians 4:8 ESV)

Do not be conformed to this world, but be
transformed by the renewal of your mind, that
by testing you may discern what is the will of
God, what is good and acceptable and perfect.
(Romans 12:2 ESV)

Why those three passages? Actually, not just those three. In fact,
the wisdom literature of the Old Testament is mirrored by the book
of James, which many theologians regard as New Testament wisdom
literature. But Proverbs 27, especially those first few verses I quoted
here, does a really great job of digging into how *not* to think. The
greater your self-loathing, the further you fall into self-righteousness,
the bigger the expanse of your anger becomes, and the harder it will
be for you to do anything positive or even to see anything as positive.
So when I say to leverage positivity, understand that I am not saying
to live passively in a positive mood. Positivity is an active lifestyle of
passionately pursuing joy. As pastor and author John Piper puts it in

his book *Desiring God*, "The deepest most satisfying delights God gives us through creation are free gifts from nature and from loving relationships with people."

And if Proverbs, especially Proverbs 27, is how *not* to think, how then should we think? This is where Philippians 4:8 comes in. It is literally a list of what to focus your mind on. And while the passage itself is long and full of excellent ideas—things that are pure, lovely and commendable for example—the most important clue in the text is at the end: "if there is anything worthy of praise." If you think you have found anything besides God that is worthy of praise, focusing your mind on it ultimately will either point to God as the source or be revealed as an unworthy example.

Earthly leaders often receive praise for what they do in one field or another, yet you might think very differently of them if you knew the truth underneath it all. There is often some secret layer—perhaps the person is secretly an adulterer, has a drug addiction, beats their children, or worse. Even if you start from a list only of people in Christianity, you'll cross paths with the sinful nature of humanity. Mother Theresa, considered a saint by the Catholic Church and arguably one of the most peaceful, loving human beings in my lifetime, kept a journal that revealed inner frustrations that paint her in a less than saintly light. In *Mother Theresa: Come Be My Light*, many of the letters she wrote express her frustrations with people and even with God and shed light on her as a person wrought with struggle. And that's OK. In her sinful nature, she petitioned the Catholic Church to destroy those letters, and they denied the request. Our natural inclination is to hide our sin, the same way that when Adam and Eve realized they were naked, they hid themselves with fig leaves (see Genesis 3:7 NIV). So to Mother Theresa sought to hide the sins she knew were in that journal of her inner most thoughts from the world.

If you begin a list of events, situations, or things your find praiseworthy, no matter what the list contains, it only takes a moment of reflection to be reminded that we are to praise the gift-giver, not the gift. At first you may think that "the giver" is a person or nature or something, but in the end I suspect you will recognize it's God. So if we agree that the only truly praiseworthy individual is God, what should you set your mind on?

Once you are reminded of God being the focus of praise and therefore the focus of our thoughts, the logical next step in this three-passage leveraging of positivity is Romans 12:2. "Do not be conformed" to what the world tells you is attractive or what it says success is. God made you, and He set you upon every step you've taken, so don't look down upon anything in your life. It is nothing other than the sovereignty of God at work, so be glad for it.

I know what I just said may be a tough pill to swallow, but it is necessary to choke it down. The sovereign grace of God alone is your salvation. Anything that was hard in your life was meant to carve you more into the image of His Son and is therefore worthy of praise as an experience. In focusing on Him and His will, you are leveraging positivity. It isn't supposed to be an instant fix. It doesn't mean things are going to be hunky-dory all the time. It means that by fixing your eyes on Him always, you'll be able to be joyful and positive, and that will be the leverage you need to make it through day to day.

God does desire your prosperity, but the end result of that desire, the true and final analysis of what He is working out in you, is changing you into the image of Him, and that involves growing pains. That's OK because the prosperity He's holding for you is the one and only thing worth working for. The single greatest treasure ever is eternity in His presence, with His Son and free of sin. Being "transformed by the renewal of your mind, that by testing you may discern what is the will of God" will involve difficulty, but rather than coming into conflict with the prosperity He wants for you, that difficulty is precisely the means by which He is leading you towards prosperity. Not giving more to the church, though God desires that you tithe. Not praying more, though God desires that you pray. He is driving the ship, and He knows exactly where to take you to reach the prosperity He has in mind for you. You need to trust Him, trust His process, to surrender to His will.

And in saying that, I pull off a bandage. If we are to submit to the power of His will, what about *our* willpower?

Think about it

1. What can you do to "let someone else praise you"? How could you accomplish that to leverage positivity?

2. Paul's list of things to focus on in Philippians 4:8 is great! How often do you find yourself focusing on these things instead of worries or negative things? How could you shift your mindset to leverage your positivity?

3. How are you conformed to this world? And how could you make a change today to leverage your positivity?

4. Do you think if you were able to leverage positivity, you could gain prosperity in the way God intends for you?

The Power of Will

As I begin this chapter, it's important to address a tremendous gaping chasm we fall into when we use the word "willpower." And not because willpower, in and of itself, is a bad concept. The challenge in exercising willpower is not to get lost in the fallacy of thinking it's about us. Remember, we may think we are the main characters in a story about ourselves when in reality we are supporting characters in a story about God. When we focus on our own will, we are in essence saying that we have the final word in the matter—that our will be done so that our kingdom, or the way we want things to be, can come. Prosperity theology often uses phrases such as "name it and claim it" and "manifestation" to teach people that through an exercise of the mind and the will, they can get whatever they want, reducing God to a genie they have mastered. But that's not how God tells us it is in the scriptures. The actual way of things is that the Cross has the final word.

Our prayer, taught to the disciples as the example for all of us by Jesus Himself is that, "Thy kingdom come, Thy will be done on earth, as it is in heaven" (Matthew 6:10 KJV). His will for us is that He be glorified in our actions. Our fall into sin took us away from rightly glorifying Him in our actions but, because of Christ, didn't separate us from Him forever. We just tend to mean well but somehow still miss the point. The English word *sin* translates the Old Testament Hebrew חָטָא (*chata*) and the Greek New Testament ἁμαρτία (*hamartia*), both of which originally meant to 'go astray' or 'miss the mark.' By focusing on our will, we point ourselves in the direction of our heart. Charles Spurgeon, the English Baptist preacher renowned by many denominations as the Prince of Preachers, asserted that "the greatest enemy to human souls is the self-righteous spirit which makes men look to themselves for salvation." If we work to our own ends, we miss the point entirely.

So what do we do to thwart the need to assert our will? Let me unpack just a little bit more of the concept itself. I don't want you to think that your willpower is a bad thing. Having willpower is not bad. We were made in His image, and if we were without will, we would be a blemished reflection of our Creator. It's a matter of design versus direction. God made all things, and therefore all things are inherently good. But we can take the things made for good and use them sinfully. Fire, for example, was made to warm us on cold nights, cook our food, and cast light in the evening hours when the sun is down. But fire can be, and frequently is, used to cause death and destruction.

The concern we ought to bear in mind is whether what we desire is in line with what God desires—that is, God's will. We cannot be trusted to make choices based solely on our will: "The heart is deceitful above all things and beyond cure. Who can understand it?" (Jeremiah 16:9 NIV). Prosperity gospel wraps itself firmly around a person's desire—the expectation that if we are aligned with the right behavior patterns, we can enact our will or have it delivered upon us.

One of the passages of scripture used most heavily by prosperity preachers is "and I will do whatever you ask in my name, so that the Father may be glorified in the Son" (John 14:13NIV). Taken at face value, it seems to support prosperity gospel assertions. But Jesus isn't known to be a fan of material things, and what he says specifically is that you must ask *in his name*. Originally his name was to be Emmanuel (Matthew 1:23), which means "God with us." The implication then is that if you ask for something in *your* name, like a sweet new ride, a promotion, the winning lottery numbers, or a perfect life partner, you may get it if it is God's will—but you certainly won't get it simply because you will it to be so. But ask for something in His name, and you might pray to be a lighthouse that shines hope and love to those who need, or salt and light for the glory of God and the building of His kingdom, or an image bearer as we are called to do from the first day of human existence, when God says we were created in His image (Genesis 1:27). We are to carry His name with truth and purity, not throw shade on Him by taking His name in vain (Exodus 20:7 KJV). This taking of His name in vain is often misinterpreted to mean cursing, but it would be better translated as *carry* the Lord's name in vain. If we are image bearers carrying His image around with us, to do so in vain would be to act in a way that does not properly illustrate to the gentile world what He is like. So not loving God and your neighbors *is* taking His name in vain.

If we think that we can will our lives to be something or include something we want, the chances are not bent in our favor. When we pray for guidance, for purpose and direction, for a way to be of service to those abused, distressed, or in pain, we will see it done in our lives. And the greatest reward we could possibly hope for would be showered upon on us from within by the Holy Spirit. We'll be blessed with the soul-satiating joy that can come only from a life lived with and for Him in service. When I broke down the gospel in Chapter 4 into the four Cs—creation, corruption, crucifixion, construction—the last part, after our salvation (crucifixion), comes as we are changed by the Spirit from within and respond to that grace in service (construction). That, my friends, is His will and is without doubt what Jesus meant in John 14:13.

So maybe now you're thinking, as I often do, "Yeah, I get it, our plans aren't His plans, but how do I even know what on earth to do, and if it's my will or His that I'm serving?" It's a good question, and I have to answer it in two ways. The first way may not be too helpful: I have no idea. It would be arrogant of me to say that I have figured out a way to understand the divine game plan, and super arrogant to say that I could tell you that plan. But the second answer, the way I'm excited to share with you now, is that it comes down to faith, prayer, and practice.

Faith

Ephesians 2:8 (NIV) tells us that faith is paramount, "for it is by grace you have been saved, through faith—and this is not from yourselves, it is the gift of God." This scripture means two things to us: faith is a quality found in those who are saved, and faith is not something that we do for ourselves. We don't decide to have faith and then get saved. We would never choose God on our own. Space does not permit for me to properly explain the doctrine of Total Depravity which is what that last sentence is grounded in, but for the sake of clarity, it can be summarized this way: It's not in our nature as post-Genesis 3 (vv1-7, the passage in the Bible where we eat the fruit and first fall into sin) human beings to choose something other than ourselves. We inherently self-orient as a result of the Fall. We chose to eat the fruit because we were promised that it would make us "like God," and even though we were already made in His image, and thus as close to being like Him as we could be, we thought that eating it would make us *more* like God. What it actually did is make us think we were as good as He was, and so we could be His equal and do what He does. If we think we are His equal, there is no reason to choose God.

So God chooses us, and He did so from the beginning. He chooses us, the Spirit works in our hearts, and we come to Him through faith. That faith is then the vessel by which God's grace showers upon us in Christ. We see His work in our lives by having faith. Our faith draws us near to Him. Having faith helps us to remember who's in charge, and it's not us. We remember and we seek him every day in faith.

Prayer

Prayer is a central focus of the Christian life. It is our one-way conduit to God, the way in which we speak to Him. That isn't to say that it is a one-way conversation by any means, God speaks to us in a variety of way. I simply mean that it is direct to Him, without detours or loop holes. We see Jesus praying to God the Father many times in scripture. In the gospel of Luke alone, Jesus prays five times

(Luke 3:21; 5:16; 6:12; 9:18, 28). He teaches his disciples what prayer should be like in Luke 11. Philippians 4:6 (NLT) tells us, "Don't worry about anything; instead, pray about everything. Tell God what you need, and thank him for all he has done." In prayer we can find the gratitude for life that is often lacking, especially when we don't have all the luxuries we wish for.

> Rejoice always, pray without ceasing, give thanks in
> all circumstances; for this is the will of God in Christ
> Jesus for you. (1 Thessalonians 5:16-18 ESV)

The prayer life we grow in helps us keep our hearts open to God's leading. We surrender our problems to Him in prayer. We pour out our feelings to a God who listens and understands through prayer. We ask for help for ourselves, our families, and our friends through prayer, and we acknowledge and ask that the Lord's will be done.

Practice

Finally we come to application. Having a regular prayer life is a discipline. Turning from sin and repenting is a daily struggle. We must constantly remember to orient our hearts, thoughts, and actions towards Christ. The Spirit is at work in our lives, crafting from the inside to work towards making our outside reflect the image of Christ. This process is *sanctification*, and it is something that we are constantly experiencing through the work of the Holy Spirit. It is lived out in our conversations, in our work ethic, in personal and professional relationships, in our marriage, and in the ways we serve our community and church. It shows itself in the way we treat our kids, the way we care for our bodies, the way we care for our planet.

We aren't expected to be perfect, and these things we do aren't what saves us. It is "not by works, so that no one can boast" (Ephesians 2:9 NIV) that we are saved. We do these things because we are saved. The salvation we receive is because God chose us (See Romans 8:30) and because He chose us, He saved us, and now that we are saved the work He prepared for us can be done for His glory. It is a response, out of gratitude for being saved. It's important to note that these works come *after* we are saved, not before. If we did them before, we could be confused that God liked us because we did good things for Him, and so He chose us as a result. there are schools of thought that support this, but I will say in short order here that I don't believe that, and I don't believe the Bible supports it either.

Now because we have salvation in Christ, we get the opportunity to build His kingdom through these actions that are placed on our hearts, "for we are God's handiwork, created in Christ Jesus to do good works, which God prepared in advance for us to do" (Ephesians 2:10). We are doing exactly what He has planned for us to do. We are living exactly what He has for us to live. We are His handiwork because He is the main character, and He gets to decide, not the other way around. So when we make large donations to the church because the pastor said that doing so will save us, that pastor is not preaching the gospel. Ephesians clearly tells us that it isn't *our* efforts that save us.

And if our deeds don't save us, our words certainly aren't saving us either. In declaring power statements such as "I am successful" and the like, we are no more controlling the outcome than if we simply stayed mute. We can't declare our way to heaven. We can't declare ourselves righteous. It's generally a good idea to stay positive, and Paul tells the church in Ephesus, "Rejoice in the Lord always: and again I say, Rejoice." (Ephesians 4:4 NIV). But the idea of the power of positive thinking and speaking positivity into your life should not be confused for biblical truth.

Think about it

1. How do you feel about surrendering your will to God? Do you think you can trust His will for your life?

2. How does your faith directly impact your willingness to surrender to God?

3. What would you pray for today with regard to God's will?

4. Do you believe that the prosperity gospel is correct that you can will things into being, like "I am successful?" Do you believe that is what God's definition of prosperity is for your life?

This prayer is so powerful and representative of the heart-posture we need to have in order to fully embrace the concept of surrender, which I shared with you also in chapter 2. True surrender is an issue of perspective and is fundamental to the gospel. If you can see that the Lord who created the universe is also creating your story, then you should also be able to see the need for you to surrender to the process. It's hard to do that, I know, so before you scoff at this page and close the book in frustration, let's take some time to talk through it.

I wasn't always so convinced of this perspective. I was in my own world, living my own story, and it wasn't working out so well. I can't stress enough that while prosperity gospel would have you believe giving to the church and praying a ton will orient God to your wants and needs so that He'll give you what you desire, it simply does not happen that way. There is an orientation of will, but it is your will that needs to be oriented towards His. Surrender the things you think you want, sit down at the cross each morning, and pray to God—then you will be where He wants.

The further I get from the person that I was, the clearer this becomes. So let me be frank: there will be times when you think God isn't there for you. There will be times when you see hardship in your life and prosperity in other people's lives, and you'll want to shout "What about me?" You want to scream at the sky that it isn't fair. And it is in those times that the Lord is nearest to you. It is the perspective you take towards the hardship that makes all the difference. It's right in the moment you're struggling through that you need to remember that Christ *gets it*. He knows you are struggling. He understands your frustration. He went through the worst suffering you can imagine. He underwent torture that was literal, visceral, and mind-numbing. He was crucified for you. He gets it. He gets the hurt you're feeling. When he ascended to heaven, he didn't return to a pre-incarnate state.

He remained in his humanness. He stayed in a state that kept Him close to us. He remains tethered to us in a real, tangible way.

Society has all sorts of cute sayings that are unhelpful, like "turn that frown upside down" and "it's all good." They're not bad thoughts. But they don't *do* anything for you. Instead of lame phrases like "just look on the bright side," focus on the fact that the Lord Jesus Christ, the author and perfecter of our faith, did for you the one thing you could never do yourself. He conquered sin and death for you. And the rest of it, no matter what hardship you currently face, is only a temporary part of an eternal life that you get to live in the presence of God. So repeat after me (perhaps in your head if you're around people right now): "I will not tell myself silly things to fluff my self-centeredness. I will instead ask myself, 'What is God trying to say to me through this?'"

Repeating that to yourself you will not instantly get more focused. It won't make anything better about your situation. But I will say this with 100 percent certainty: by focusing on God in the midst of your struggle, you will draw nearer to Him, and that in and of itself makes it better. And while you are dealing with the beginning, middle, and end of something truly awful in your life, also think of the words of Spurgeon: "It is not how much we have, but how much we enjoy that makes happiness."

Think about it

Before answering these questions, turn back to the beginning of the chapter and read John Wesley's prayer again.

1. What is your current perspective on your life? Are you the main character? Or God's supporting character?

2. When you've been through a tough time, have you had success shifting your perspective to God? How could that have helped?

3. When things are hard, it can be difficult to find things to enjoy. What could you do to make that easier? How can you practice this technique today?

4. Do you think this shift in perspective would help you prosper?

5. What do you think of the Spurgeon quote that closed this chapter, and how does "having" versus "enjoying" make a difference in your life?

10

Influenced

Before I get too invested in talking about influence, I want you to look at an image.

Take a really close look at the two faces. Which is bigger, the face on the left, or the one on the right? Don't measure; just react.

What facts can we determine?

+ Both faces are circular.
+ Each face has two eyes and a mouth.
+ One face has a light background with a dark face.
+ One has a dark background with a light face.
+ One is smiling.
+ One is frowning.

Have you decided which one's bigger? Did you first think it was the happy face and then change your mind? Or were you sure it was the sad face and now are unsure? Did you maybe think right off the bat that they are the same size?

I've made this demonstration dozens of times over the last several years at real estate conferences, Christian schools, youth groups, a car dealership, hair salons, and all sorts of other groups, and the results are always the same. About half of the people in the room believe that the images are the same size. About 30 percent say the sad face is bigger, and about 15 percent say the happy face is bigger. There is always a group of people that say the faces are the same size, though that number is totally random and I've never been able to get a proper percentage, though it typically ranges between 20-40 percent of the room.

Now I know that many of you are doing the math right now and thinking "That doesn't equal 100 percent" or "Wow, there are some really dense people in those rooms." The truth is that most people don't answer. All people form an answer I'm sure, they just keep it to themselves. So what if someone in your group of friends was sitting with you and they told you that they are positive that one of them is definitely bigger? Or what if I told you that after discussing it amongst themselves, and with my leading a discussion about it, nearly all people eventually chose the same side of the image? Don't stress your brain too much on this, I'll come back to it later. For now, just take away this idea: that peers, presenters and messages of all kinds can and do influence us to think and behave a certain way. People who started with the right answer to the image often changed their minds after discussing with their peers.

The only real way to know for sure the right answer is to measure it. Which I asked you not to do. But measuring is the right way to handle things that we are trying to properly understand or interpret. The means by which we measure something vary depending on what it is, but all things have a measurement. When trying to figure out if a pastor or Christian author is teaching something that aligns with God's word, the measuring stick is God's word.

People are often indecisive when faced with what should be obvious. When the Bible says something like, "Delight yourself in the LORD, and he will give you the desires of your heart" (Psalm 37:4 ESV), we might readily understand that to mean whatever your heart desires, He will give you. But consider that God's desire is for us to turn from sin, to turn to Him, and to Glorify Him in all that we do. If I desire in my heart of hearts to rob a bank so I can have tons of cash to blow on gambling, drugs, and women, I think it very unlikely that He is on board for that, whether I delight in Him or not.

That was an extreme example, so let's turn to a more down-to-earth one. If I delight in the Lord but want the nicest car and an overflowing bank account, I'm being covetous and actually not delighting in God at all. To truly delight in God is to be grateful for what has been given to you, not to have a list of things you want or worry about wanting. Rest on the fact that He will provide what you need, or take it a step further and realize that all you actually need is Him. That's the measure of whether you are in line with what that passage was saying. Scripture interprets scripture. So if a particular passage seems unclear, you can trust that the Bible has other examples of that lesson that will clarify, and with the tools available to us today, it wouldn't take long at all to find other biblical references to trusting in God in order to figure out the pasage. We are told clearly by Jesus Himself:

> "Therefore I tell you, do not worry about your life, what you will eat or drink; or about your body, what you will wear. Is not life more than food, and the body more than clothes? Look at the birds of the air; they do nor sow or reap or store away in barns, and yet your heavenly Father feeds them. Are you not much more valuable than they? Can any one of you by worrying add a single hour to your life? And why do you worry about clothes? See how the flowers of the field grow. They do not labor or spin. Yet I tell you that not even Solomon in all his splendor was dressed like one of these. If that is how God clothes the grass of the field, which is here today and tomorrow is thrown into the fire, will he not much more clothe you—you of little faith? So do not worry, saying 'What shall we eat?' or 'What shall we drink?' or 'What shall we wear?' For the pagans run after these things, and your heavenly Father knows you need them. But seek first his kingdom and his righteousness, and all these things will be given to you as well." (Matthew 6:25–33 NIV)

God will provide for you what you need, and your heart, changed by the Holy Spirit, should desire Him. Seek first His kingdom. Why then do we believe that He will give us whatever we want? Because we are told that we should be allowed to want anything and that we should be able to have it all. You see gurus on social media all the time telling you that you can easily and quickly get to your first six-figure paycheck. I did a quick search on Amazon.com, and there were over two thousand books on how get rich quickly for less than $10. With just the click of a button I can have my pick of thousands of inexpensive ways to "guarantee" the life of my dreams.

There are three circles of influence that we are a part of regularly. There is a secular aspect to them, but also embedded within our contemporary Christian faith is the influence of prosperity gospel. The Bible tells us, "let us throw off everything that hinders and the sin that so easily entangles. And let us run with perseverance the race marked out for us, fixing our eyes on Jesus" (Hebrews 12:1b–2a NIV). Identifying the three circles of influence is the fastest way to be on the right side of the influencing. Those three circles are your community, your friends and family, and yourself, and though there are many other spheres of influence, these three are the most tangible. I'll be unpacking all three but in this chapter let's look at just the first two. The third and most specific of the circles has a chapter all to itself.

Community

When you go out of your house and enter into your community, you are being influenced. Magazines are full of "you're not good enough because you aren't XYZ" articles. Movies and TV shows are full of startlingly attractive women who, we are led to believe, just come by that naturally or with little to no effort, or maybe they have busy lives (as if they don't have the luxury of childcare or a personal assistant or a self-dictated schedule) but can always squeeze in the gym. And those women play alongside the six-foot-four square-jawed man's man with chiseled abs and a sensitive side who knows just what to say all the time, loves puppies and long walks on the beach, casts long romantic gazes into his partner's eyes, and showers her in presents. The only prominently large areas of the woman's body are the sexual parts, and the only thing the man can't lift, fix, or do is find true love.

And even if that isn't the kind of life we want, we somehow still feel inadequate. I've never had chiseled abs, and I've never had the cash to shower my wife in gifts. I've never expected my wife to be anything like those women. Her soul-piercing eyes, infectious laugh, and fierce love for Jesus will always make her more attractive than anything else in this world to me. And even if she knows I feel that way, I wager she feels the influence of those worldly magazines and movies and feels inadequate at least once in a while.

We are told where we should eat, what we should wear, what kind of car to drive, how big a house to have and how to decorate it—I mean, for goodness' sake, we even get influenced into making our Starbucks order into some artisanal, bougie expression of our inner coffee lover, even if our inclination is to ask for it in basic black, or maybe cream and sugar.

I am not above it, my wife isn't, and my kids aren't. Neither is my pastor, who happens to be one of my best friends and the most insightful man I know. And you probably aren't either.

The Bible tells us, "You are the light of the world. A town built on a hill cannot be hidden. Neither do people light a lamp and put it under a bowl. Instead they put it on its stand, and it gives light to everyone in the house. In the same way, let your light shine before others, that they may see your good deeds and glorify your Father in heaven" (Matthew 5:14-16 NIV). So how do we turn it around?

I'm not saying it's easy, but if we just remember that there is a right way and a wrong way, and Christ is the right way, it helps a lot. If you know the right way, then you can rest in the fact that you have eternal life: "For it is by grace that you have been saved, through faith" (Ephesians 2:8a NIV), That is amazing news—life-altering news that you should be shouting from the rooftops.

Do you like jokes? I like jokes a lot. Let me tell you one.

A CrossFitter, a vegan, and an essential oiler walk into a bar ... and everyone knew about it.

For those of you whose sense of humor differs from mine, I'll explain. How did everyone know about it? Because if you are a vegan, or if you do CrossFit or use essential oils, you tell people. Like, every person you encounter. You wear clothes that cleverly announce it. You carry tumblers with logos from your favorite brands, or you bring your own food along. Clearly this is a caricature, but it does in fact describe a type of person that everybody seems to know. If someone feels that becoming part of a group or movement has changed their life for the better, they often share the news and try to convert people to that way of life. We do the same thing when we see a movie we loved, eat at a great restaurant, or when we finish binge watching a show on Netflix. We. Tell. Everyone.

Yet for whatever reason, as Christians we keep it to ourselves that the God of the universe undeservedly gave us eternal salvation. Isn't that life-changing enough to warrant discussion? How do we become the influencer instead of the influenced? Gandhi famously said it best: "Be the change you wish to see in the world." Don't force your beliefs down people's throats, but also don't be ashamed. Paul opens the book of Romans (Romans 1:16) by exclaiming that he is not ashamed of the gospel, and you shouldn't be either. Talk about it. *Talk about Jesus with everyone.*

Friends and Family

It stands to reason that the people closest to you would have the greatest influence on you. Your wife or husband, siblings and parents, and nearest and dearest friends (in that order, usually) are the ones who can and often do cause the largest sway in a person's beliefs and behaviors. Your spouse doesn't want to watch your favorite show, so you don't watch the show—or at least not when you want to. Your parents don't like certain foods, they don't make certain foods, and therefore you end up not liking those foods. Of course, people go against the influence of their parents all the time—in fact, we are called to move out from their influence: "Therefore a man shall leave his father and his mother and hold fast to his wife, and they shall become one flesh" ().

This passage from Genesis shines a light on the influence of your spouse. If you are of one flesh, how could you possibly disagree? So maybe not at first, but at some point in your marriage, you begin to make slight, perhaps imperceptible, and most definitely subconscious adjustments to your personality. Your spouse does the same.

I'm writing this chapter from an Airbnb during a youth leadership conference. As we came into town yesterday, we stopped for gas. While waiting in line to buy a sweet tea, I overheard a conversation that I think perfectly illustrates the influence of your friends. I'd been struggling with finding an example for this section—truth be told, I don't have a ton of friends. I spend most of my time at home with my beautiful wife and three awesome kids. I'd been praying for the friendship example that was eluding me and working on other chapters in the meantime, but leave it God to give you just what you need.

> SHADRACK. Hey, I'm feeling like watching a movie and grabbing dinner at that new Thai place. Wanna join?
>
> MESHACK. Nah, I'm not feeling like Thai. You guys go.
>
> ABENDIGO. I've already seen everything that's playing.
>
> SHADRACK. Come on, it'll be fun. It's not like you have anything else going on tonight.
>
> ABENDIGO. Why don't we run through Chick-fil-A and go shoot pool?
>
> MESHACK. That sounds good. Love me some of God's chicken.
>
> SHADRACK. OK, cool. Sounds like fun.

It made me smile, and I've given them all names from the Bible because it made me smile more. But you see how easily we are influenced? Shadrack was sold on his plan of dinner and a movie. He tried to influence the group to do what he wanted, but within fifteen seconds his entire agenda for the night had changed—and he was looking forward to it.

Now what if you were told by your closest pal that God was sold on your having a million dollars? That is, if you want wealth, He wants it for you. Such a God can deliver people into your life who could easily give you that promotion you want, the car you're lusting for, the house of your dreams. You don't need to feel guilty if that sounds fantastic!

I quoted Psalm 37:4 above ("Delight yourself in the LORD, and he will give you the desires of your heart"), and there are dozens of similar examples in both the Old and New Testaments. You may have a friend who decided to turn his life around and read books like *How to Win Friends and Influence People, 7 Habits of Highly Effective People* and *The 10X Rule*—all great books. But if he's decided what he wants and can achieve all of that, it isn't a stretch to imagine that friend getting God into the mix: "I can do all things through Christ who strengthens me" (Philippians 4:13 NKJV). A statement like that can make us feel superhuman, as if we can make all our dreams come true. But then if, or more likely when, that doesn't play out, a common response is that instead of concluding the books weren't right, we look at the authors and think, "It *must* work because it works for them."

As sinful, broken people, we look for someone to blame. And who do so many people land on? It's either blame yourself or blame God. If you blame yourself, you fall into a downward spiral of self-deprecation, and on some level you grow resentful of yourself, thinking something along the lines of "If everyone else can do it, why can't I?" And then it isn't a long leap from that to "something must be wrong with me." Or if you don't blame yourself, the blame may land on God. If "I can do all things through Christ," but I wasn't able to do the things I set out to do, then one of two things must be true: either God doesn't love me, or God isn't able to do all things. Because both of these are horribly wrong, I have come to believe that prosperity gospel is the fastest path to a lost faith in Christ, faster than any other false gospel or opposing religious viewpoint out there right now.

How do you become the influencer among your immediate family and friends? I don't have the answer, but Jesus teaches us exactly what our plan ought to be:

> "Therefore everyone who hears these words of mine and puts them into practice is like a wise man who built his house on the rock. The rain came down, the streams rose, and the winds blew and beat against that house; yet it did not fall, because it had its foundation on the rock." (Matthew 7:24–25 NIV)

Jesus's teachings are pretty straightforward, if you slow down and really listen to them. Just put those beautiful words of His into practice. He gives us the simple instruction to love God and love people: "Love the Lord your God with all your heart and with all your soul and with all your mind and with all your strength. The second is this: Love your neighbor as yourself. There is no commandment greater than these" (Mark 12:30–31 NIV).

Is that actually simple? Of course not! But it's something you can work towards. And if you are working towards it with the sanctification of the Holy Spirit, those closest to you will see it. They will see the difference in you, and they will want to know what the deal is. Evangelism at its finest is the act of being changed by God in Christ in view of the public. Being secretive does nobody any good. And if you keep quiet about it, you'll open yourself up to those who aren't. And when the loudest voice isn't Jesus, you can so easily get confused.

Before we get too far away from it, I have to make just a quick clarifying statement. I've said "influencer" a couple of times now. That term is used most often to refer to social media or brand influencers and while I didn't mean to reference them (I mean influencer literally as in "*someone who influences is an influencer*") I can't help but address the perfect irony. The "influencer" on Facebook, Instagram, Youtube or wherever is precisely the wrong voice to let speak loudest. Listen to God, let His word speak loudest to your mind and your heart.

Think about it

1. How does your community influence you? Are you happy with that, or are there aspects you wish didn't influence you? How could you make changes?

2. Which of the three circles are you most influenced by? Do you have other circles of influence?

3. How do your friends and family influence you? How could you influence them?

4. How can you lead by example to be an influencer in other people's circles?

Influencing

The innermost of the three circles of influence I outlined in the previous chapter, the circle that is largest of the three in level of importance but also smallest in scope, is *you*—you yourself. You influence yourself more than anyone else. It is a gift from God that we have that self; without it, we are lacking in free will and therefore not capable of giving or receiving love in the way that the God who is love intended it to be. He gave us the sense of self that we all have so that we can respond to His love with our love. We are made in His image so that we can respond the way he would.

But that sense of self made a mess of things. Genesis 3 kicks off with a banger of a conversation between a talking serpent and Eve. The serpent, more crafty than any of the wild animals God made (Genesis 3:1a NIV), played right into Eve's sense of self. He said something to her that we regularly tell ourselves: you can do it yourself. He influenced her into eating from the one tree God commanded man not to eat from, and thus sin entered into our being and spread throughout the world. As you read through Genesis, by the time you get to the account of Noah sin has fully encapsulated everything. For the first generation of mankind, it was a simple act, a bite of a fruit we were told never to eat. The very next generation, it was murder. There was a steep and steady increase from generation to generation to the point that today we don't even see sin—it's just a part of things.

I hear people all the time today saying things like, "The enemy is whispering in your ear" or "The devil made me do it." To me, there is no bigger crime we commit against ourselves than to pass the blame on to the serpent, as Eve did (Genesis 3:13). It is our brokenness that causes us to bend ever so slightly towards the sin in a given situation. The devil may be sly, he may be influential, but it is our predisposition towards our sinful nature that ultimately cause us to go with the wrong choice. And let's be honest with ourselves: when we make those errors in judgment, often we know it's wrong. Paul puts it this way: "They show that the law is written on their hearts, while their conscience also bears witness, and their conflicting thoughts accuse or even excuse them" (Romans 2:15 NIV). We know it's wrong because God placed what's good and just and right, like an amazing tattoo from heaven, smack dab on the center of our hearts.

But it is our very nature to go against Him. And so you may be wondering, if it's my nature to sin no matter what, then how on Earth can I influence myself to do any different? Your one and only hope is to surrender your life to Jesus.

I know that sounds like you cannot influence yourself, but the truth of the matter is, trying to do it on your own is a fool's errand.

We aren't capable of lifting ourselves up from the muck and mire on our own. That's the powerful lure of prosperity gospel: we can work hard and improve our status, since God wants our success and will give it to us. But it is only the transformative power of the Holy Spirit that can really change us. So in order to control the influence you have over yourself, give yourself over to Him. Study His word, pray to Him, and know that He is there working things out for your good and His glory. Gratitude and a heart of thankfulness will always be better than anger, frustration, or disappointment about things we do or do not have.

Don't be so blind as to believe you are destined to have it all just because you decide one day that you want it all and are going to work hard for it. Pastor and author Paul Tripp once said, "Hope is not found in telling yourself you have the wisdom and strength you need, but in remembering God has graced you with all you need." The real prosperity in Christianity is that God has given us everything we could possibly need: salvation in His Son, Jesus Christ. The rest of it, the stuff we want so deeply to have and feel prosperous in possessing, amounts to nothing but distraction, idols that take our eyes off the God whose unyielding love for us is fully satisfying to those chosen to receive it.

Has the 2 faces image in the previous chapter been bothering you? I told you I would circle back to it and here we are. The answer to which one is bigger is that they are exactly the same. The point of the exercise is that we are all susceptible to influence on some level. Maybe the image didn't fool you even for a second. Whether or not it did is less important than the idea itself. It challenges many, many people even if in the end they chose to stick with their original feeling that the faces are the same. The point is this, Even the firm foundation-standing, hand-raising, knee-bending, Bible-reading, Sunday-serving Christian can fall victim to the influence of the secular world and its mentality that hard work and firm belief can get you anything. And when that belief gets too far into your brain, you start hearing prosperity gospel and thinking it makes perfect sense. Next thing you know, you're buying *The Secret* and trying to manifest your best life, all the while thinking you deserve it because you are a good Christian.

You don't deserve it. I don't either. No one does. What we have, all that we have, is a freely given gift of God's grace. And that we can't deserve.

So let yourself be influenced—but by God, as revealed to us in His Word. Align yourself with scripture and hold steadfast to it. Do not let the world influence you. We are meant to be *in* the world but not *of* it., at the end of His life, Jesus prayed:

> I have given them your word and the world has hated them, for they are not of the world any more than I am of the world. My prayer is not that you take them out of the world but that you protect them from the evil one. They are not of the world, even as I am not of it. Sanctify them by[d] the truth; your word is truth. As you sent me into the world, I have sent them into the world. For them I sanctify myself, that they too may be truly sanctified. (John 17:14–19 NIV)

He is doing all the work, sanctifying us through the power of the Holy Spirit because we are not of this world. Own that and believe it with all of your being. Allow yourself to be influenced by the Spirit who is inside us all, changing us from the inside out to resemble Jesus Christ, our Savior.

Think about it

1. Do you have a tendency to pass the blame when you're caught in your sin? How can you change that reaction?

2. What does it mean to you to surrender your life to Jesus? How exactly would you go about doing that? Or if you've already done it, how would you tell someone else to do it?

3. What distractions do you have in your life that take your eyes off God?

4. How do you think God's influence in your life could help you to prosper?

12

Generosity

Our culture has a lot to say about money. It isn't just pieces of paper; now it's imaginary numbers represented and disbursed by a piece of plastic. But we make it of utmost importance. John Calvin famously said that "the human heart is an idol factory." And oh, man, was he right.

If you asked a prosperity gospel preacher (who likely wouldn't take kindly to being called that) what God wants for us, you might hear something like, "God wants you to have it all" or "Name it and claim it, and the Lord will provide." In fact, those are actual quotes from renowned prosperity preachers I found online. Typically, it is followed with a call for tithes and offerings, as it was in both these cases. In transitioning to offerings, preachers will say that the Bible calls us to give back, and maybe discuss generosity in Christian life. At my church, it's often explained that you are leaving a financial offering, but it is meant to be a token of a larger and more impactful commitment. You're saying to God, "I'm returning to you this small portion of what you have blessed me with as a token to represent my entire life, which I also give to you as my offering. I give you my life, all my time, talents, and treasures, because I know that I have them only because you ordained it so." It's a beautiful moment, recognizing as you put your check or cash into the offering plate or box, or click submit for your digital offering, that you belong to Him and that you surrender all of yourself to Him.

At the website The Gospel Coalition, Chris Cagle lists five myths Christians tend to believe about money. The fourth myth made life so much easier for me that I wish I'd read it earlier in my walk with Christ:

> God will prosper me financially if I work hard and have enough faith.
>
> Historically there have been two perspectives on financial prosperity and the Christian life. The first teaches that because love of money is the root of all evil (1 Tim. 6:10), the more money you have, the less righteous you can be. The second teaches that God wants all Christians to be prosperous and wealthy. If we aren't prosperous, it's because we don't have enough faith.
>
> A more accurate biblical perspective is that God in his sovereignty gives some people more, and others less, to steward on his behalf (1 Sam. 2:7; Matt. 26:11). How and why he does so is His business,

not ours. Mature believers may be either rich or poor
(Prov. 22:2).

I love this explanation. It is vibrantly clear to me that God is in
control of things, and for me to think that my faithfulness has any
impact on Him gives me way too much credit.

The truth is, we don't bring anything to the table in our
relationship to God except for our need. You can't help but see,
though, that people who have awful habits or terrible lifestyles are
making big money, and you the faithful Christian are living paycheck
to paycheck, or worse. I get it. But take comfort in Jesus's words:

> "So when you give to the needy, do not announce it
> with trumpets, as the hypocrites do in the synagogues
> and on the streets, to be honored by others. Truly
> I tell you, they have received their reward in full."
> (Matthew 6:2 NIV)

We aren't supposed to be boastful about our tithing, just as
we aren't supposed to be boastful about anything, but the part
I want you to key in on is the conclusion: "Truly I tell you, they
have received their reward in full." What He's saying is twofold:
first, these people are not honoring God in the way we are called
to; second, they are getting the very best they're ever going to get
right now in this life.

Am I saying they aren't doing what they're supposed to, but they
get to the big rewards? Actually, the opposite. Remember the earlier
discussion about what we really ought to be focused on? The world
exists as it is now, full of fallen men and women like you and me. But
that world will pass away one day, and we will all be called to account.

We are immortal beings living a mortal experience right now, and while they might get all the riches of the world for a time, you as a child of God will get your reward in heaven: eternity with the Father. So let them have their fun now, because in a hundred years they will be nothing but a memory, and you will be united with His Glory, seeing Jesus in His perfection, living with Him forever. Talk about treasure, my friend—that is worth treasuring, and you have a seat at that table by faith in Him who's called you.

The prosperity or reward that the people are receiving in the verse from Matthew just above is the same prosperity that successful non-Christians of today are getting. I think John Piper may have framed it best in a Twitter post of July 6, 2012, when he said that "prosperity cannot be proof of God's favor, since it is what the devil promises to those who worship him." It's what the devil offered Jesus in the wilderness:

> Again, the devil took Him [Jesus] to a very high mountain and showed Him all the kingdoms of the world and their glory. "All this I will give You," he said, "if You will fall down and worship me."
>
> "Away from Me, Satan!" Jesus declared. "For it is written: Worship the Lord your God and serve Him only." (Matthew 4:8-10 NIV)

All the kingdoms of the world and all their glory? That is the ultimate prosperity. To own all the things of the earth. That was the last and final of Satan's temptations, and it was the biggest. It was his long shot. But what can you offer the One who holds the world already?

81

We don't need prosperity to know that God loves us. We don't need wealth to know that He cares for us. Our Savior willingly died in the most excruciating way possible so that we could be reunited with our Father in heaven. That is a kind of love that is undeniable, and it leads to an unfathomable prosperity in the kingdom of heaven for thousands of lifetimes and beyond. I know that money may make it easier, or seem to. But let's say Jesus Himself was standing in front of you, with Peter, James, and John in tow. Before you can get a word out, Peter says, "You my brother (or sister), will be dirt poor and struggle all the days of this life so that He may be glorified with our Father in heaven." Would you even bat an eye before consenting? But because He isn't in the flesh standing before you, and you're being asked to take your situation in faith, is it a whole different story?

No, it isn't different, or at least it shouldn't be. Give because you are called to. The money didn't belong to you in the first place—it belonged to the Lord. Remember the scenario in chapter 6 about someone giving you $20 but asking you to buy him a soda? Here is where that comes full circle. God gave you all that you have. The blessing of anything and everything you own is owing to Him and His sovereignty. Pay it back to Him in spades for all that He has done and is doing in your life—not because you want something in return, not because you *have* to, but because you *get* to as a response to the incredible life change He has gifted you with.

Earlier in this chapter, I quoted Matthew 6:2 to talk about people who are given their riches now. Later Jesus goes on to say,

> "Do not store up for yourselves treasures on earth, where moth and rust destroy, and where thieves break in and steal. But store up for yourselves

treasures in heaven, where moth and rust do not
destroy, and where thieves do not break in and steal.
For where your treasure is, there your heart will be
also." (Matthew 6:19–21 NIV)

Jesus is giving us a heavy dose of instruction here; heavy, because it is not at all what we want to hear. Storing up treasures here on Earth is doable. We can work hard and earn money. We can invest well, spend well, live thoughtfully, and end up with wealth and financial security. And we should do those things, if we want to. His point isn't that we should not have anything here because we have it waiting for us a million times over in heaven. His point is that if we focus our hearts and minds on what we have waiting for us, which He is storing up for us because He loves us, then what we have here won't matter. It won't bring us stress, it won't bring us joy. It will simply be.

The end of this passage carries with it a grave warning that is often glossed over, especially in prosperity gospel preaching: "for where your treasure is, there your heart will be also." If you are focused on your treasures here, your heart will be here also. And our hearts cannot be oriented in two directions at once. We are either of the flesh or of the spirit. If your heart is here on earth with your treasure, then you, like the hypocrites whose reward has been given to them in full, will get all your reward here too. And if that sounds awesome, go back a few pages and start reading again, because my friend, you missed something.

The deception found in prosperity preaching is a hard one in this instance, and that's why it's so pervasive in our culture. It is preached that God wants you to prosper and that tithing more will create in turn a willingness in God for you to prosper. But it's about where your heart is, not about the tithing. God already has a willingness for you to prosper. But *He* defines prosperity, and He sets the timeline.

I know this from experience. It wasn't so many years ago that for a time I simply did not make enough money to cover all my bills. I had lost my job, I was struggling in my family life, and all I really had was Jesus. I had only just given my life to Him, so I was in a rough place. I knew I wanted to be fully committed, to fully submit to Him. So when I heard my pastor preach about generosity and tithing, I thought, "OK, if I give 10 percent, we will have to tighten up elsewhere. But the kids don't know what our finances are, and my wife is with me on this journey, so let's do it." And so I gave 10 percent out of every check. Sometimes more than 10 percent, but never less. And you know what? Somehow all the bills got paid.

Things got easier over time, and today all the bills still get paid. But it didn't happen overnight. Tithing, giving to the church for the building of His kingdom, is not a give-and-take scenario. It is not an exchange. You give because He gave it to you first. You are taking a posture of reverence and gratitude for having received in the first place. He then looks after you in ways that you couldn't possibly do yourself and couldn't possibly understand. Be generous with your money, but also with your time and your talents too. Help other people and build them up whenever you can.

This might not sound like God leaning into you to make you prosper, but that is exactly what it is. Through community, through fostering a servant heart, you will experience prosperity. Just remember to define prosperity through God's eyes, not your own, because as I've said repeatedly, it isn't about you. There is a monumental difference between your pastor saying, "We are called to give our resources back to the Lord" and your pastor saying, "Give, because the more you give, the more God will bless you, heal you, and prosper you." The first will orient you towards God; the second gets you thinking falsely that you can orient God towards you.

Think about it

1. Do you find it difficult to tithe? Why or why not?

2. What do you expect from God when you tithe?

3. Are you bothered or comforted by the fact that your faithfulness doesn't have any influence on God?

4. How do you think giving of your time and finances can help you prosper?

So What Do I Do Now?

If you have made it this far, I first want to say thank you. You went on this journey with me and didn't get to a point where you decided to throw this book out or burn it and curse at me as the author, or at the very least, you didn't put it down and stop reading. (Maybe you felt like it at times?)

Anyway, as you are reading this last chapter, I want to make sure that in the midst of all we unpacked, you have something tangible to walk away with. This book was meant to do two things: look at the prosperity gospel from multiple angles, and provide you with the biblical foundation for the concept of prosperity. In digesting all that, the goal was for you to see the sovereignty of God in your life and to know without a doubt that we are not the center of attention, not the center of the universe, not the main character. The subtitle of this book asks you to consider what your story is. We are in fact part of the redemptive story that God is writing. This is His story, and we are blessed to be supporting characters.

If I've done a reasonably good job of making my case up till this point, then what I'm about to say might be a "duh" moment for you. And even if I haven't done a great job, I hope this will not be an earth-shattering revelation at this point.

The prosperity gospel cannot stop Jesus.

Prosperity gospel preachers will not interfere with God's plan. And you, by taking the time to read this book, are at the very least curious enough about the truth of the gospel to dig deeper when someone says that God will make you wealthy or that they can heal you in the name of Jesus.

Jesus knows that people will do things in His name that He isn't supporting. He even says,

> "Not everyone who says to Me, 'Lord, Lord,' will enter the kingdom of heaven, but he who does the will of My Father who is in heaven *will enter.* Many will say to Me on that day, 'Lord, Lord, did we not prophesy in Your name, and in Your name cast out demons, and in Your name perform many miracles?' And then I will declare to them, 'I never knew you; Depart from me, you who practice lawlessness.'" (Matthew 7:21–23 NIV)

The best part is that we aren't the ones meant to wage war against them. Christ is. We are called to live faithfully to Him and to go and make disciples in all nations by teaching people the true gospel of

Christ through relationships (Mathew 28:19–20, 2 Timothy 2:2).
So that means all you have left to do is to follow the two greatest
commandments, to "love the Lord your God with all your heart and
with all your soul and with all your mind … and Love your neighbor
as yourself" (Matthew 22:37, 39 NIV) and to "be on your guard
[and] stand firm in the faith" (1 Corinthians 16:13a NIV). When
faced with those who are preaching "prosperity," be courageous in
proclaiming the true gospel. Trust in the Lord for your life. Believe
that He has your best interests at heart. And when things get really
tough, don't ask God why. Ask yourself what you can learn from the
place God has you in right now.

If you take away anything from this book, it should be this: God
is good all the time. If your situation doesn't feel like He is being good
to you, it isn't because you aren't tithing enough or praying enough.
We do not influence God by our actions. The situations we each find
ourselves in are the result of our narrow understanding of His plan
for our lives.

To put it another way, we see only the part of the story we are
currently living, not the conclusion. We don't even see the conclusion
of the chapter, much less the entire book. There's no way we could
possibly understand what He is doing—that's part of the deal. That's
the faith we are called to have: faith in Him to lead our steps, and
faith that He will help us to be faithful.

I fully believe that He is helping us. That He is guiding our
steps. That He is good and trustworthy and faithful and kind and
loving, and that He does want us to prosper. His Son's death on the
cross sealed the deal for our prosperity because it reunites us with
the Lord in a relationship that sin tore apart and that no action of
ours could ever bring back together. That doesn't mean we prosper in

the here and now. But this isn't all we have. We have eternity in His beautiful presence, and that is the kind of prosperity that we should really pray for.

Think about it

1. After finishing the book, how would you define prosperity now, and how does that definition differ from when you started?

2. Have you ever asked God why? Did you get an answer? What do you do in those frustrating times? And has this book better equipped you to understand them?

3. Do you agree that prosperity gospel is harmful to the message of Jesus?

4. How do you feel about letting God be the main character and being secondary to His story?

5. As you move on from this book, what is the tidbit you're hoping to hold on to most? What are you praying for?

May the grace of our Lord and Savior Jesus, and May the love of God and the fellowship of His Holy Spirit be with you in your journey to spread His truth. Amen.

Scriptures Cited

Passages are listed in order of appearance in the text and meant here to be used as a reference in case you don't have a bible handy while reading a page of this book that references a biblical text but doesn't quote it.

Jeremiah 17:9 (ESV): "The heart is deceitful above all things, and desperately sick; who can understand it?"

1 John 2:15–17 (ESV): "Do not love the world or the things in the world. If anyone loves the world, the love of the Father is not in him. For all that is in the world—the desires of the flesh and the desires of the eyes and pride in possessions—is not from the Father but is from the world. And the world is passing away along with its desires, but whoever does the will of God abides forever."

John 20:29 NIV: "Because you have seen me, you have believed; blessed are those who have not seen and yet have believed."

Matthew 4:4 NIV: It is written: Man shall not live on bread alone, but on every word that comes from the mouth of God.

Exodus 16:1-5 NIV: The whole Israelite community set out from Elim and came to the Desert of Sin, which is between Elim and Sinai, on the fifteenth day of the second month after they had come out of Egypt. In the desert the whole community grumbled against Moses and Aaron. The Israelites said to them, "If only we had died by the Lord's hand in Egypt! There we sat around pots of meat and ate all the food we wanted, but you have brought us out into this desert to starve this entire assembly to death." Then the Lord said to Moses, "I will rain down bread from heaven for you. The people are to go out each day and gather enough for that day. In this way I will test them and see whether they will follow my instructions. On the sixth day they are to prepare what they bring in, and that is to be twice as much as they gather on the other days."

1 Timothy 6:17–19 NIV: "Command those who are rich in this present world not to be arrogant nor to put their hope in wealth, which is so uncertain, but to put their hope in God, who richly provides us with everything for our enjoyment. Command them to do good, to be rich in good deeds, and to be generous and willing to share. In this way they will lay up treasure for themselves as a firm foundation for the coming age, so that they may take hold of the life that is truly life."

John 3:16 NIV: "For God so loved the world that He gave His one and only Son, that whoever believes in Him shall not perish but have eternal life."

Matthew 28:19 NIV: Therefore go and make disciples of all nations, baptizing them in the name of the Father and of the Son and of the Holy Spirit

Psalm 23:4a ESV: "Even though I walk through the valley of the shadow of death, I will fear no evil, for you are with me."

Matthew 5:12 ESV: "Rejoice and be glad, for your reward is great in heaven, for so they persecuted the prophets who were before you"

Matthew 4:8–9 NIV: "Again, the devil took him to a very high mountain and showed him all the kingdoms of the world and their splendor. 'All this I will give you,' he said, 'if you will bow down and worship me.'"

2 Timothy 2:2 NIV: "And these things which you have heard me say in the presence of many witnesses, entrust to reliable people who will be qualified to teach others."

Genesis 3:8–13, 21 NIV: "Then the man and his wife heard the sound of the Lord God as he was walking in the garden in the cool of the day, and they hid from the Lord God among the trees of the garden. But the Lord God called to the man, 'Where are you?' He answered, 'I heard you in the garden, and I was afraid because I was naked; so I hid.' And he said, 'Who told you that you were naked? Have you eaten from the tree that I commanded you not to eat from?' The man said, 'The woman you put here with me—she gave me some fruit from the tree, and I ate it.' Then the Lord God said to the woman, 'What is this you have done?' The woman said, 'The serpent deceived me, and I ate.' … The Lord God made garments of skin for Adam and his wife and clothed them."

Genesis 6:5 NIV: "Every inclination of the thoughts of the human heart are only evil all the time."

Genesis 6:5 NLT: "The LORD observed the extent of human wickedness on the earth, and he saw that everything they thought or imagined was consistently and totally evil."

John 1:14a KJV: "And the Word was made flesh, and dwelt among us."

Romans 8:28 NIV: "And we know that in all things God works for the good of those who love him, who have been called according to his purpose."

Romans 15:13 NIV: "May the God of hope fill you with all joy and peace as you trust in him, so that you may overflow with hope by the power of the Holy Spirit."

John 10:10 NIV: "The thief comes only to steal and kill and destroy; I have come that they may have life, and have it to the full."

Matthew 16:24–26 ESV: "Then Jesus told his disciples, 'If anyone would come after me, let him deny himself and take up his cross and follow me. For whoever would save his life will lose it, but whoever loses his life for my sake will find it. For what will it profit a man if he gains the whole world and forfeits his soul? Or what shall a man give in return for his soul?'"

Matthew 7:13–14 NIV: "Enter through the narrow gate. For wide is the gate and broad is the road that leads to destruction, and many enter through it. But small is the gate and narrow the road that leads to life, and only a few find it."

Matthew 7:15 NIV: "Watch out for false prophets. They come to you in sheep's clothing, but inwardly they are ferocious wolves."

Jeremiah 17:9 NIV: "The heart is deceitful above all things, and desperately sick; who can understand it?"

Genesis 6:5 NIV: "Every inclination of the thoughts of the human heart is all evil all the time."

Galatians 5:19–25 NIV: "The acts of the flesh are obvious: sexual immorality, impurity and debauchery; idolatry and witchcraft; hatred, discord, jealousy, fits of rage, selfish ambition, dissensions, factions and envy; drunkenness, orgies, and the like. I warn you, as I did before, that those who live like this will not inherit the kingdom of God. But the fruit of the Spirit is love, joy, peace, forbearance, kindness, goodness, faithfulness, gentleness and self–control. Against such things there is no law. Those who belong to Christ Jesus have crucified the flesh with its passions and desires. Since we live by the Spirit, let us keep in step with the Spirit."

Matthew 20:28 NIV: "…just as the Son of Man did not come to be served, but to serve, and to give his life as a ransom for many."

Mark 10:25 NIV: "…For even the Son of Man did not come to be served, but to serve, and to give his life as a ransom for many."

John 13:1-17 NIV: It was just before the Passover Festival. Jesus knew that the hour had come for him to leave this world and go to the Father. Having loved his own who were in the world, he loved them to the end.

The evening meal was in progress, and the devil had already prompted Judas, the son of Simon Iscariot, to betray Jesus. Jesus knew that the Father had put all things under his power, and that he had come from God and was returning to God; so he got up from the meal, took off his outer clothing, and wrapped a towel around his waist. After that, he poured water into a basin and began to wash his disciples' feet, drying them with the towel that was wrapped around him.

He came to Simon Peter, who said to him, "Lord, are you going to wash my feet?"

Jesus replied, "You do not realize now what I am doing, but later you will understand."

"No," said Peter, "you shall never wash my feet."

Jesus answered, "Unless I wash you, you have no part with me.""Then, Lord," Simon Peter replied, "not just my feet but my hands and my head as well!"

Jesus answered, "Those who have had a bath need only to wash their feet; their whole body is clean. And you are clean, though not every one of you." For he knew who was going to betray him, and that was why he said not every one was clean.

When he had finished washing their feet, he put on his clothes and returned to his place. "Do you understand what I have done for you?" he asked them. "You call me 'Teacher' and 'Lord,' and rightly so, for that is what I am. Now that I, your Lord and Teacher, have washed your feet, you also should wash one another's feet. I have set you an example that you should do as I have done for you. Very truly I tell you, no servant is greater than his master, nor is a messenger greater than the one who sent him. Now that you know these things, you will be blessed if you do them.

Luke 16:10 NIV: "Whoever can be trusted with very little can also be trusted with much, and whoever is dishonest with very little will also be dishonest with much."

Malachi 3:10 ESV: Bring the full tithe into the storehouse, that there may be food in my house. And thereby put me to the test, says the Lord of hosts, if I will not open the windows of heaven for you and pour down for you a blessing until there is no more need.

Leviticus 27:30-33 ESV: "Every tithe of the land, whether of the seed of the land or of the fruit of the trees, is the LORD's; it is holy to the LORD. If a man wishes to redeem some of his tithe, he shall add a fifth to it. And every tithe of herds and flocks, every tenth animal of all that pass under the herdsman's staff, shall be holy to the LORD. One shall not differentiate between good or bad, neither shall he make a substitute for it; and if he does substitute for it, then both it and the substitute shall be holy; it shall not be redeemed."

Hebrews 7:1-10 NIV: For this Melchizedek, king of Salem, priest of the Most High God, met Abraham returning from the slaughter of the kings and blessed him, and to him Abraham apportioned a tenth part of everything. He is first, by translation of his name, king of righteousness, and then he is also king of Salem, that is, king of peace. He is without father or mother or genealogy, having neither beginning of days nor end of life, but resembling the Son of God he continues a priest forever.

See how great this man was to whom Abraham the patriarch gave a tenth of the spoils! And those descendants of Levi who receive the priestly office have a commandment in the law to take tithes from the people, that is, from their brothers, though these also are descended from Abraham. But this man who does not have his descent from them received tithes from Abraham and blessed him who had the promises. It is beyond dispute that the inferior is blessed by the superior. In the one case tithes are received by mortal men, but in the other case, by one of whom it is testified that he lives. One might even say that Levi himself, who receives tithes, paid tithes through Abraham, for he was still in the loins of his ancestor when Melchizedek met him.

Matthew 6:26 CEV: "Look at the birds in the sky! They don't plant or harvest. They don't even store grain in barns. Yet your Father in heaven takes care of them. Aren't you worth much more than birds?"

Romans 8:28 NIV: "And we know that in all things God works for the good of those who love him, who have been called according to his purpose."

Matthew 26:52 NIV: "'Put your sword back in its place,' Jesus said to him, 'for all who draw the sword will die by the sword.'"

1 Thessalonians 5:16–18 NIV: "Rejoice always, pray continually, give thanks in all circumstances; for this is God's will for you in Christ Jesus."

Proverbs 27:1–2, 4 NIV: "Do not boast about tomorrow, for you do not know what a day may bring. Let someone else praise you, and not your own mouth; an outsider, and not your own lips … Anger is cruel and fury overwhelming, but who can stand before jealousy?"

Philippians 4:8 ESV: "Whatever is true, whatever is honorable, whatever is just, whatever is pure, whatever is lovely, whatever is commendable, if there is any excellence, if there is anything worthy of praise, think about these things."

Genesis 3:7 NIV "Then the eyes of both of them were opened, and they realized they were naked; so they sewed fig leaves together and made coverings for themselves."

Romans 8:30 NIV: And those he predestined, he also called; those he called, he also justified; those he justified, he also glorified.

Romans 12:2 ESV: "Do not be conformed to this world, but be transformed by the renewal of your mind, that by testing you may discern what is the will of God, what is good and acceptable and perfect."

Matthew 6:10 KJV: "Thy kingdom come, Thy will be done on earth, as it is in heaven."

Jeremiah 16:9 NIV: "The heart is deceitful above all things and beyond cure. Who can understand it?"

John 14:13 NIV: "And I will do whatever you ask in my name, so that the Father may be glorified in the Son."

Matthew 1:23 NIV: "The virgin will conceive and give birth to a son, and they will call him Immanuel (which means 'God with us')."

Genesis 1:27 NIV: "So God created mankind in his own image, the image of God he created them; male and female he created them.

Exodus 20:7 KJV: "Thou shalt not take the name of the LORD thy God in vain; for the LORD will not hold him guiltless that taketh his name in vain."

Ephesians 2:8 NIV: "For it is by grace you have been saved, through faith—and this is not from yourselves, it is the gift of God."

Genesis 3:1-7 NIV: Now the serpent was more crafty than any of the wild animals the Lord God had made. He said to the woman, "Did God really say, 'You must not eat from any tree in the garden'?" The woman said to the serpent, "We may eat fruit from the trees in the garden, but God did say, 'You must not eat fruit from the tree that is in the middle of the garden, and you must not touch it, or you will die.'" "You will not certainly die," the serpent said to the woman. "For God knows that when you eat from it your eyes will be opened, and you will be like God, knowing good and evil." When the woman saw that the fruit of the tree was good for food and pleasing to the eye, and also desirable for gaining wisdom, she took some and ate it. She also gave some to her husband, who was with her, and he ate it. Then the eyes of both of them were opened, and they realized they were naked; so they sewed fig leaves together and made coverings for themselves.

Luke 3:21 NIV: When all the people were being baptized, Jesus was baptized too. And as he was praying, heaven was opened

Luke 5:16 NIV: But Jesus often withdrew to lonely places and prayed.

Luke 6:12 NIV: One of those days Jesus went out to a mountainside to pray, and spent the night praying to God.

Luke 9:18 NIV: Once when Jesus was praying in private and his disciples were with him, he asked them, "Who do the crowds say I am?"

Luke 9:28 NIV: About eight days after Jesus said this, he took Peter, John and James with him and went up onto a mountain to pray.

Luke 11:1-4 NIV: "'Father, hallowed be your name, your kingdom come. Give us each day our daily bread. Forgive us our sins, for we also forgive everyone who sins against us. And lead us not into temptation.'"

Philippians 4:6 NLT: Don't worry about anything; instead, pray about everything. Tell God what you need, and thank him for all he has done.

1 Thessalonians 5:16-18 ESV: Rejoice always, pray without ceasing, give thanks in all circumstances; for this is the will of God in Christ Jesus for you.

Ephesians 2:9 NIV: not by works, so that no one can boast.

Ephesians 2:10 NIV: For we are God's handiwork, created in Christ Jesus to do good works, which God prepared in advance for us to do.

Ephesians 4:4 NIV: "Rejoice in the Lord always: and again I say, Rejoice."

Psalm 37:4 ESV: "Delight yourself in the LORD, and he will give you the desires of your heart."

Matthew 6:25–33 NIV: "Therefore I tell you, do not worry about your life, what you will eat or drink; or about your body, what you will wear. Is not life more than food, and the body more than clothes? Look at the birds of the air; they do nor sow or reap or store away in barns, and yet your heavenly Father feeds them. Are you not much more valuable than they? Can any one of you by worrying add a single hour to your life? And why do you worry about clothes? See how the flowers of the field grow. They do not labor or spin. Yet I tell you that not even Solomon in all his splendor was dressed like one of these. If that is how God clothes the grass of the field, which is here today and tomorrow is thrown into the fire, will he not much more clothe you— you of little faith? So do not worry, saying 'What shall we eat?' or 'What shall we drink?' or 'What shall we wear?' For the pagans run after these things, and your heavenly Father knows you need them. But seek first his kingdom and his righteousness, and all these things will be given to you as well."

Hebrews 12:1b–2a NIV: "Let us throw off everything that hinders and the sin that so easily entangles. And let us run with perseverance the race marked out for us, fixing our eyes on Jesus."

Matthew 5:14–16 NIV: "You are the light of the world. A town built on a hill cannot be hidden. Neither do people light a lamp and put it under a bowl. Instead they put it on its stand, and it gives light to everyone in the house. In the same way, let your light shine before others, that they may see your good deeds and glorify your Father in heaven."

Ephesians 2:8a NIV: "For it is by grace that you have been saved, through faith."

Romans 1:16 NIV: For I am not ashamed of the gospel, because it is the power of God that brings salvation to everyone who believes: first to the Jew, then to the Gentile.

Genesis 2:24 NIV: "Therefore a man shall leave his father and his mother and hold fast to his wife, and they shall become one flesh."

Philippians 4:13 NKJV: "I can do all things through Christ who strengthens me."

Matthew 7:24–25 NIV: "Therefore everyone who hears these words of mine and puts them into practice is like a wise man who built his house on the rock. The rain came down, the streams rose, and the winds blew and beat against that house; yet it did not fall, because it had its foundation on the rock."

Mark 12:30–31 NIV: "Love the Lord your God with all your heart and with all your soul and with all your mind and with all your strength. The second is this: Love your neighbor as yourself. There is no commandment greater than these."

Genesis 3:1a NIV: Now the serpent was more crafty than any of the wild animals the LORD God had made."

Genesis 3:13 NIV: "Then the LORD God said to the woman, 'What is this you have done?' The woman said, 'The serpent deceived me, and I ate.'"

Romans 2:15 NIV: "They show that the law is written on their hearts, while their conscience also bears witness, and their conflicting thoughts accuse or even excuse them."

John 17:14–19 NIV: "I have given them your word and the world has hated them, for they are not of the world any more than I am of the world. My prayer is not that you take them out of the world but that you protect them from the evil one. They are not of the world, even as I am I of it. Sanctify them by[d] the truth; your word is truth. As you sent me into the world, I have sent them into the world. For them I sanctify myself, that they too may be truly sanctified."

1 Timothy 6:10 NIV: "For the love of money is a root of all kinds of evil. Some people, eager for money, have wandered from the faith and pierced themselves with many griefs."

1 Samuel 2:7 NIV: "The LORD sends poverty and wealth; he humbles and he exalts."

Matthew 26:11 NIV: "The poor you will always have with you, but you will not always have me."

Proverbs 22:2 NIV: "Rich and poor have this in common: The LORD is the Maker of them all."

Matthew 6:2 NIV: "So when you give to the needy, do not announce it with trumpets, as the hypocrites do in the synagogues and on the streets, to be honored by others. Truly I tell you, they have received their reward in full."

Matthew 4:8–10 NIV: "Again, the devil took Him [Jesus] to a very high mountain and showed Him all the kingdoms of the world and their glory. 'All this I will give You,' he said, 'if You will fall down and worship me.' 'Away from Me, Satan!' Jesus declared. 'For it is written: Worship the Lord your God and serve Him only.'"

Matthew 6:19–21 NASB: "Do not store up for yourselves treasures on earth, where moth and rust destroy, and where thieves break in and steal. But store up for yourselves treasures in heaven, where moth and rust do not destroy, and where thieves do not break in and steal. For where your treasure is, there your heart will be also."

Matthew 7:21–23 NIV: "Not everyone who says to Me, 'Lord, Lord,' will enter the kingdom of heaven, but he who does the will of My Father who is in heaven *will enter*. Many will say to Me on that day, 'Lord, Lord, did we not prophesy in Your name, and in Your name cast out demons, and in Your name perform many miracles?' And then I will declare to them, 'I never knew you; Depart from me, you who practice lawlessness.'"

Matthew 28:19–20 NIV: "Therefore go and make disciples of all nations, baptizing them in the name of the Father and of the Son and of the Holy Spirit."

2 Timothy 2:2 NIV: "And the things you have heard me say in the presence of many witnesses entrust to reliable people who will also be qualified to teach others."

Matthew 22:37, 39 NIV: "Love the Lord your God with all your heart and with all your soul and with all your mind ... and Love your neighbor as yourself."

1 Corinthians 16:13a NIV: "Be on your guard [and] stand firm in the faith."

Psalm 55:22 NIV: "Cast your burden on the Lord, and he will sustain you; he will never permit the righteous to be moved."

Printed in the United States
by Baker & Taylor Publisher Services